Lester Roloff
In
Life
And In
Death

A Gift For:
Bro. Finley Crutchaw

From: Wayne & Joyce Moon

Bro. Finley,
Thank you for your faithfulness
and firm stand for Christ.
Loved in Christ,
Bro. Wayne
Phil. 1:6
10-12-97

Lester Roloff
In
Life
And In
Death

Marie Brady Roloff
Bobby R. Glenn

Family Altar
Publishers

Published by Family Altar Publishers
A Division of Roloff Evangelistic Enterprises, Inc.
P.O. Box 1177
Corpus Christi, Tx   78403

Printed in the United States of America

Acknowledgement

Lester Roloff — In Life And In Death

For my part of this book, I am deeply indebted to my wife, Eleanor. If it were not for her patience, inspiration, and proofreading, this book would not have been possible. Miss Ida Cavitt, Mrs. Irene Smith, and Mrs. Martha Green have also provided an invaluable service in proofreading assistance. Mr. Melvin Roloff and Mr. Edell Roloff were an inspiration to me because of their willingness to spend much time telling stories about the Roloff boys' upbringing. I am also indebted to Belinda Geliske, Laura Glenn, and Debra Glenn for their patience while their parents were out of circulation.

—Bobby Glenn

Dedication

Lester Roloff — Living By Faith

This book is lovingly dedicated to the memory of my precious husband, our two dear daughters, our eight grandchildren, and to our parents, Mr. and Mrs. H. A. Roloff and Mr. and Mrs. S.W. Brady, who have gone to be with the Lord.

— Marie Brady Roloff

Introduction

The original idea of the Board of Directors of the Roloff Evangelistic Enterprises was to print a book covering the last years of Lester Roloff's life. Then, the realization came that such a book would not be clearly understood by the readers unless they were close to the ministry or had read Mrs. Roloff's earlier book which was entitled *Lester Roloff — Living By Faith.*

The decision was then made to reprint her book, after making revisions and corrections, and make it a part of a larger book that would cover Brother Roloff's entire life.

It is imperative that a great number of the youth of America catch the spirit of dedication to the will of God which this man had — even in his early years.

Lester Roloff's life quest was to discover and emulate the ministry, message, and methods of Jesus Christ. To that end, he prayed much, studied diligently, and memorized volumes from the Word of God.

God honored his faith.

Much of the book is prayerfully intended to reveal to the parents of today's youth, and to the youths themselves, what went into the makings of this vibrant man of God. May there be some who will see from this man's life that Jesus Christ is worthy of their total faith and service.

If there is one who reads this book who has never come to a saving knowledge of the Lord Jesus Christ — there would be no greater joy than to hear that you have given your heart to the Savior. You can be one additional trophy to God's glory that can be traced to the grace of God as it was manifested through the human instrument — Lester Roloff.

— Bobby R. Glenn

Contents

Part Three: *In Life And In Death*
Bobby R. Glenn

Part One

Lester Roloff — In Life And In Death
Bobby R. Glenn

1

Makings of a Man of God

> Some years ago I came face to face with a man
> I called the most unusual Christian in the world
> — that man was Lester Roloff. He was stern
> and uncompromising when dealing with sin but
> was loving and compassionate when dealing
> with the worst of sinners. He was bold as a
> lion when facing the evil world but humble as
> a child when he came into the presence of the
> Lord.
>
> Dr. Lee Roberson (1994)

Lester Roloff was offered honorary doctorate degrees,
accolades, honors, and awards from Christian organizations
all over the nation. The special recognition was for standing
firm for convictions he received from God's Word, the *Holy
Bible.* He was chosen by Bob Jones University to receive its
1974 "Founder's Award for Defending the Scriptures."

The National Religious Broadcasters inducted Brother

Roloff into their Hall of Fame posthumously at their 1993 Convention in Los Angeles, California. During the presentation banquet, Stuart Epperson said, "Brother Roloff had a backbone of steel and a heart of gold."

When one man heard of the recognition Lester was receiving, he asked, "Why is it so unusual that someone would stand firmly for the convictions God has given him?" Why is that not said about every ambassador of Christ? After the much publicized stand-off with the state of Texas in their drive to close the Rebekah Home for Girls in 1979, one *Corpus Christi Caller Times* news reporter had this to say about him:

Every official — from the Nueces County Attorney to the Governor of Texas to justices of the U.S. Supreme Court — has condemned him for his stubborn refusal to accept the state licensing they say his homes must have. Yet to thousands of Americans, Lester Roloff is a hero cut from the cloth of men like the biblical prophet Daniel or Texas patriot Jim Bowie. As they see it, he is a man of unbending convictions, a stalwart guardian of U.S. Constitution's guarantee of religious freedom. For 35 years his radio audience has remained devoted to Roloff, sending money to support his enterprises and providing foot soldiers to fight in what he calls his war against state encroachment on the church. Controversy has never been stranger to the 64-year-old preacher. He has felt the heat and outlived it many times during the past quarter century.

Why did this man not waver in his convictions, and why did he have the strength to stand for those convictions against what seemed at times to be the whole world? What made him different? There is total agreement that this man was indeed different from most preachers, pastors, and evangelists. Many reasons for this difference are discovered as one searches methodically into his life. True experiences in the life of this phenomenal man make very interesting stories; some touch your heart, others are humorous, most are unique.

In searching for something to explain the cause for the difference in his life, let us first look at the mature man. Aside from his intense ministry, was there anything unusual about his actions, appearance, or mannerisms that would give us a clue as to why God used him in an extraordinary way?

He was five feet, ten inches tall, this man, and when one sat across the desk from him, there was an awareness of square shoulders but nothing that hinted of great physical strength. He had quick, penetrating blue eyes, receding blond hair, and a square jaw. When he stood, his back was honor-guard straight. His arms rarely hung loosely by his sides. His hands were large for his frame but amazingly adroit. His fingers were nimble. He listened attentively as one spoke. He was witty and laughed easily. He asked questions often. A compassionate heart swiftly brought tears of empathy. He was not one to waste time in trivial chatter, but his countenance was always kind. There was something about his swift and sincere smile that built confidence even in a defeated dope addict. Gestures and bodily movement highlighted his calm articulate speech. He was always busy with a current project or in planning the next. Outwardly, he seldom seemed completely relaxed. He was not a saunter-ing man; he walked briskly. He was keen, clever, and intense. He disciplined himself in daily Bible meditation and scripture memorization. Often his conversations and confer-ences ended with prayer; he would stand and pray or go to one knee. If a matter was a particularly heavy burden to him or a visitor, he might lie on the floor as he prayed for God's help in the matter at hand; he always prayed in Jesus' name.

From this brief description, nothing notable stands out except prayer and Bible study; nothing explains the cause for his unbending dedication to convictions for which he lived and died.

The obvious answer is that God gave him the convictions along with the grit to stand for them. However, that might be too simplistic. God's action often is an effect that has a cause. There are scriptural precedents that reveal God's special interest in young people whose lives show unusually high character. The following are examples: Joseph, Moses, Daniel, Samuel, David, and the three Hebrew youths — Shadrach, Meshach, and Abed-nigo.

Was there a reason behind the choosing of Lester Roloff other than God's own sovereign will? If so, will He make it known now to sincere and seeking Christians? What caused him to love the down-and-out people enough to push himself unmercifully in raising the millions of dollars necessary to shelter, clothe, and feed them? What was the source of his tenacious resistance to the attack on his youth ministry by the Texas Department of Human Resources and the news media?

The people to whom he ministered were rejected and unwanted by society; why was he driven to introduce them to Jesus? Why was he so devoted to seeing them transformed into happy, moral, and productive Christian citizens? What made him give all of his own resources, including a large inheritance, into such a selfless cause? What made him work from twelve to sixteen hours almost every day in this business of rescuing humanity's rejects? As his brother Melvin says graphically, "Lester gave his life for people no one else would spit on." In a ministry such as his, the competition was conspicuous by its absence. Is it possible to discover the makings of this man? Can a cause for such dedication be found in his roots, childhood, or adolescence? Were the major contributing factors his guidance and education?

Many sincere Christians did not understand why Brother Roloff took such a strong stand against the state's quest for control over the youth rescue ministry of the church. No funds were received from the state. Certainly, such governmental actions were not intended by the writers of the First Amendment to the United States Constitution. This amendment was the first of the eight amendments which became known as the "Bill of Rights." It reads: *Congress shall make no law respecting an establishment of religion, or prohibiting the free exercise thereof.* This amendment also includes the freedom of the press. The First Amendment has been taught to school students throughout the years as the very cornerstone of our democratic process. That cornerstone is now crumbling. Brother Roloff was one of the few who had the wisdom to know that if he lost his case, the church's ministries would forever be under the threat of oversight by the government. Ask the Russians how that affected their churches.

Unquestionably, God instructs His church to help those in need. It does not matter why help is needed. Whether people need help because of poverty or because of their sins, the church is to provide the help. According to the Constitution, the state is not to make a law respecting the free exercise of this God-ordained ministry.

It might have helped some to understand Lester Roloff if they had known more about the stock from which he had come. He came from a family which had deep allegiance to God, to the United States of America, and to our great Constitution. Their allegiance to the liberty in this nation

15

was a compelling motivation simply because their grandfather had experienced the loss of liberties in his native land. Melvin explains why his grandpa came to America.

Grandpa William Roloff was born in Germany where the name was spelled "Rohloff." He left Germany because of the loss of religious liberty and every other worthwhile freedom. The conscription would have forced him into the military service to fight for atheistic ideals. He had been told that in America the liberties he held dear were constitutionally "guaranteed." He came, he observed, he stayed. His new home fulfilled his dream, and he loved it. He deeply appreciated his new-found liberty.

After settling in Wisconsin for a time, Grandpa Roloff moved to Texas and eventually bought property near Dawson, where he was affectionately known as "Uncle Billy" Roloff.

Lester's brother Edell tells a story about their grandpa that shows the deep feelings of his allegiance to America as compared to Germany.

In World War II, America, with its Allies, was fighting against the Axis forces, including the Nazis of Germany. One day during the war a man from the Dawson community, who was known there as "Uncle Jesse", was speaking from the platform at the front of a local church where Uncle Billy was in attendance. The man said, "I want all of you to know that I am a German sympathizer; I think they are right and we are wrong. America is on the wrong side in this war."

Everyone was shocked, speechless, and frozen in their seats — except Uncle Billy — whose personal experiences in Germany came flooding back into his mind.

Feelings about the Nazis were intense. He walked to the front of the church where the people of Dawson were to see the real depth of his feelings about America and his beloved freedom. They saw a fist fight in a church service. Nothing was more divisive in any community during the war than people who were unpatriotic coming up against super patriots — sparks were sure to fly. Uncle Billy and Uncle Jesse then sat on different sides of the church and refused to speak to one another. (Wouldn't it be ironic if Germany's postwar citizens eventually end up with more liberties than the postwar citizens of the United States?)

Years later a friend and I were fishing at a pond near Dawson when a fellow came riding toward us as fast as his horse would carry him.

"Have you heard the news?" he asked excitedly as he reigned in near us.

"No, what happened?" I asked.

"Uncle Billy and Uncle Jesse are friends again. During the revival service everything was made right between them. They actually embraced each other in the center isle."

That added a note of spiritual victory to a story that had become etched in the annals of the little town of Dawson.

It is obvious that there was great strength of conviction in Lester's unique heritage. It is also a lesson that Lester never forgot concerning the healing power of God to those who are willing to ask Him and each other for forgiveness.

Now, in that Central Texas town of Dawson, there is a monument built in honor of Uncle Billy's grandson, Lester, who also made a valiant stand when he saw these same freedoms, for which his grandfather was willing to fight, methodically being taken from Americans.

There will be some who say with their most pontifical look, "How unlike Christ this Uncle Billy must have been to have resorted to pugilistic means to express himself." Remember that Christ used a whip to drive people from the temple when they were using it for something that dishonored God. Defending the godless actions of Hitler's Germany might fit into that same category.

The Roloff men had strong convictions and were willing to stand for them. This was surely a factor in God's selection of Lester to stand against state encroachment on the church's liberties.

Some will surely insist that there is no explanation for God's choosing Lester because God does not respect one personality or temperament over another. True. However, it is certain that God *is* a respecter of actions, especially when those actions are motivated by faith. One of Lester Roloff's favorite chapters in the Bible was the eleventh chapter of Hebrews which he always read before the annual meeting of his Board of Directors. He continues to read that same chapter via tape recording before every annual meeting of the Board of Directors of the Roloff Evangelistic Enterprises, Inc. That chapter makes it clear that if faith is the impetus for actions, those actions will please God. *When* did God start molding Lester for future service?

In the Bible account of David, he was used in a mighty way in his calling by God. He accomplished miraculous fetes by the power of God. But when did God begin dealing with him? If God was not directly supplying the courage and strength when David killed the lion and the bear with his bare hands, He surely must have been taking note of such an unusual youngster.

In a less spectacular way, was there something notably different about Lester Roloff when he was a youngster, or is that God's secret?

It was not a secret known only to God in David's case. God wanted everyone to know the lad's unusual differences. Why did little David take on Goliath when all of Saul's army stood silently shaking behind their shields? The answer is that he was prepared mentally, emotionally, physically, and spiritually to step out by faith. Belief in God, hard work, and dedication to the responsibility given to him by his father were important factors in that training. The soldiers were clearly lacking in such preparation and dedication.

Did David know that God would guide the stone from his slingshot that would kill Goliath? Obviously not. He knew there was danger involved, or he never would have tried on Saul's armor. Five stones were chosen, not just one. He surely knew there was a risk of losing his life. When Esther yielded to God's call, she spoke for every person whom God calls for extraordinary service; she said, *"If-I-die-I-die."* God obviously called David because he was ready to be used. David shortly proved he was indisputably ready to face the unknown, all alone, for the great God of Israel.

Did David have the blessings of his family? No, his brothers ridiculed him. Did he stop because the king (government) thought his plan was foolish? No. He had a mission he wanted to accomplish for his God. He did not need the consent and applause of men.

Lester Roloff taught that a big part of faith is knowing God is pleased with the thing you are doing. He believed an acceptable service to God requires obedience to God's Word. "So then faith cometh by hearing, and hearing by the word of God" (Rom. 10:17).

Lester told the story about the little boy who was shooting into the sky on a moonlit night with his B-B gun. A man came by and asked, "What are you trying to hit, son?"

The little boy answered, "The moon."

"Don't you know you can't hit the moon?" the man chided.

"I'm coming closer than you are," he said.

Not all of the wayward youth of our nation were converted to Christ and delivered from sin through Brother Roloff's efforts. But he came much closer to that goal than his armchair critics. He said, "In the Lord's work you are not judged by your successes but by your faithfulness."

Was he influenced by his home and community environments? If so, can we pinpoint *how* they were an influence? Is it possible today to use our rear-view binoculars to find the positive factors in his early life?

2

His Youth

"Every child should have the privilege of being reared by godly parents," Lester asserted, "people like Papa and Mama — Harry and Sadie Roloff." The principles that guided Lester came primarily from his early home life. Is there something we can discover from the techniques used in his parent's home? Many things have been learned about the methodology used by Harry and Sadie Roloff. Some accounts of their role in the childhood and adolescence of their three boys, Melvin, Edell, and Lester, are classics in the innovative implementation of Bible principles.

Like David's brothers, Lester's brothers might have doubted his call from God for a while, but later they supported him. They said, "He was our favorite preacher." They might not have agreed with all of Lester's convictions, but they knew God had called him and that he was the kind of person who would give it his best. Almost everything he did, he did with all of his might. When he started something, he finished it — if humanly possible.

His brother Edell tells of a time when Lester was very young. One day Lester decided to ride the neighbor's calf. The neighbor's boys and his brothers helped him get mounted. The calf did a great job of pitching and twisting; Lester was doing an excellent job of staying aboard. The calf pitched and bucked his way over to the earthen watering pond and in one last heave pitched Lester directly into the muddy pond. Lester came up covered with mud but grinning and obviously pleased with his successful ride. Giving up was not a part of his nature.

When he was a young man, he was known to drive his car like he performed his work — full speed ahead.

Edell told about a time Lester was driving along the highway when he saw a black man hitchhiking. Some of his closest friends were black. He seemed to have a burden to see these people preserve their rich spiritual heritage. He came to a screeching stop and gave this man a ride. Later as they were speeding down the highway, Lester inquired about the man's salvation. He asked, "If you were to die tonight, do you know you would go to Heaven? Are you sure you are saved?"

"Yas, suh, I sure hope I is," the black man said as he gripped the seat and stared wide-eyed down the highway. Then the man said, "Suh, y'see thet light yonder — that'n wankin' and blankin'?"

"Yes, I see it," Lester answered.

"Well, I be git'n out there!"

Lester said often that he was colorblind. He worked with all races alike — "All people, regardless of race, must hear the gospel, or they will die and go to Hell." He was faithful to preach the gospel to all who would hear it. He said, "I preach the scripture because God said His Word would not return void but that it would accomplish its purpose."

Faith, Lester's hallmark, has always been in high demand and short supply. It will be invaluable to all parents and Christendom as a whole if something motivational can be discovered in this critical area.

Harry and Sadie (Harry called her Sally) Roloff's objectives were simply to provide godly guidance during the impressionable years of youth. Though elementary in Bible doctrine and sometimes negated for its simplicity, it is the only sure way to success in the raising of children. It has

God's written guarantee. "Train up a child in the way he should go: and when he is old, he will not depart from it" (Proverbs 22:6).

Most Christians believe *that* is surely the need of the day, but there is a problem in knowing how to blend scripture into practical training. This is the most important thing to learn from the Roloffs. They knew how to mix biblical principles into everyday life in an unforgettable way.

The method of teaching a truth and the resultant acceptance by the boys is intriguing. Guidance was promptly given the boys when either parent sensed an upcoming need in their lives. Many Bible precepts were used by the Roloffs. Many of Christ's teachings were in direct response to specific needs of the day.

Early in their lives, the boys were mostly spectators and observers. They watched as Bible principles were applied to every situation that came into the lives of their parents. The boys detected that logic did not always prevail. Selfish interests, it seemed, were not even considered when making decisions or reacting to circumstances. They watched often as their parents met the needs of neighbors both day and night. The boys watched and listened as biblical rationale was applied to every situation. They learned the old black-backed Book was the litmus which was to be applied to everything that came into their lives.

The boys were taught they were never to tell a lie. Then they learned that, besides selfish interests, there was no reason to lie. They learned selfishness is the root cause of many, if not most, sins and how that was an important factor in the fall of Adam and Eve. The important grace of selflessness was the parental example in the Roloff home.

The boys were taught with regularity; they were in church every service in either Shiloh Baptist Church or Harmony Methodist Church which were located side-by-side out in the country. Circuit-riding, part-time pastors held services in the Baptist church one Sunday and in the Methodist church the following Sunday. The Shiloh community, made up of families from surrounding farms, usually attended the preaching services. Many important principles were learned by the boys at these churches. However, the lessons that stayed with them best were taught when Papa or Mama, or even their grandpa, looked into their faces and soberly addressed some current situation where there was a moral choice to make. Frequently, the subject had already been addressed from the church pulpits or taught by the Sunday School teachers. It was reinforced by the calm, sincere, and timely exhortation of how it was to be applied in the current situation.

3

The Matter of Prayer

Miss Frances Goodman, who later married Gene Price, was Brother Roloff's secretary and organist for many of his years in the ministry. She gives some insight into a principle that was so important in guiding the man. She said, "Many mornings when I came into the office there were two deep impressions in his office sofa. These were made by his elbows in his long seasons of early-morning prayer." He was a man of prayer — not because he was seeking that reputation but because there was an inbred dependence upon God. How did his upbringing influence that quality in his life?

Uncle Billy Roloff learned the English language after he came to America. He pronounced English words distinctly and with a German accent. The Roloff men inherited their strong voices from him.

Imitating his grandfather's strong and distinct style, Lester's oldest brother, Melvin, said, "You vant to know vhy Lester had a strong dependence on prayer? I vill tell you vhy. I vill tell you a true story about Uncle Billy."

One Sunday morning Uncle Billy Roloff went into Shiloh Baptist Church. During the service and just before the usual prayer time, Uncle Billy stood up and said, "I vould like to ask you to pray vith me about something. Vone of my mules is wery sick and is not able to vork. I vant you to pray dat God vould heal my mule." Some thought that was funny and laughed. He said, "Dat is all right — I see you don't believe the same like I do. I believe dat God is interested in anything dat touches Uncle Billy's life, so, I vill pray for my own mule." He sat down. There was no more laughing. He did pray for the mule, and the mule got well.

That is just one reason Lester believed in prayer; it was a spiritual legacy left to him through his father from Uncle Billy. Lester saw in his grandfather a man who believed that God was pleased "vhen ve tell Him everything about ourselves."

Melvin tells the story about prayer that suddenly gave him years of maturity above his age of fifteen.

Our mother was sick and in the hospital in Waco, Texas, which was about thirty miles from our home in Dawson. One day I was sitting in the shade on the back porch swinging my feet off the edge when my grandfather came driving up to the house in his Hupmobile. He got out and came around to the back porch.

"How you doing, Sonny Boy?" he asked. (He always called me Sonny Boy.)

"Oh, I guess I'm doing O.K.," I replied.

He sat and looked me squarely in the eyes and solemnly asked, "Sonny Boy, are you praying for your mother? The Lord answers the prayers of little boys, too, you know. Your mother is wery sick; you know dat, don't you?"

"Yes, sir, I know she is sick," I replied.

"Sonny Boy, your mother is wery sick; she might not be coming home."

"You mean she might die?" I asked.

"Yes, Sonny Boy, your mother might die." Then he

got up and started walking away, but before he left, he looked back at his wide-eyed, fear-filled grandson and said tenderly, "Sonny Boy, you just pray for your mama."

"Yes, sir, I will do that," I said.

That got my attention. I went off by myself to a quiet place. I forget what I said, but it was probably something like this: "Our Father, Mama is sick, and You must get busy; don't let Mama die. Please, Lord, don't let Mama die! Amen."

Mama didn't die; she came home and completely recovered. But, it was something I never forgot concerning my grandfather's attitude about prayer. It also helped change my understanding about the importance of immediacy when approaching God.

The legacy left by Grandfather Roloff was reaffirmed and strengthened by Lester's father and mother. He often remarked about his mother's encouraging reminders to him: "I pray every day for my preacher-boy son."

Brother Roloff's younger daughter, Pam, said, "I would sneak into his room and listen to him pray when he thought no one was there except him and the Lord. If there had been nothing else in his life to convince me of his genuine love for the Lord and close fellowship with Him, hearing him pray was sufficient."

4

The Work Ethic

Lester Roloff was a tireless worker. To many, his name was almost synonymous with "human dynamo." "There is no way I could keep up with that man," one preacher said, "the pace he keeps is abnormally fast; yet, he is also abnormally productive." Was Lester's productivity influenced by his experiences on the Roloff farm?

Breakfast at the Roloff home was at 5:45 A.M. All of the boys were to be ready for work when they came to breakfast; they were to be on the way to the fields by 6:00 A.M. When they came in from the fields in late afternoon, they were to do all the remaining daily chores. Papa milked in the morning; Lester did most of the milking in the evening. This skill was later to have a big part in paying for his college education.

When it was time to harvest the cotton, the boys picked from daylight till dark. They were to pick as much as, or more than any of the hired hands. Melvin remembered an incident which showed that his father could be firm, and it also showed his attitude about work. This was one thing that influenced the boys later in the formation of good work habits of their own.

One day Edell, Lester, and I, along with our black friends, Homer, Buddy, and Sunno, were working in the fields. The black boys' father, Julius Barron, lived on the farm and worked for Papa. We boys were supposed to be chopping cotton which means hoeing down all weeds and thinning the cotton plants to prevent overcrowding as they matured. We began playing instead of working. Thinking Papa was thirty miles away in Corsicana, we were throwing clods of dirt and just having a big time.

To our surprise, our father came walking up the row. Papa came up behind me with a cotton stalk and dusted my britches real good. (Edell says he missed a whipping because he had gone for a jug of water.) Papa then grabbed Lester and worked him over. Then, to our surprise, he grabbed Homer, Buddy, and Sunno and gave them the same treatment.

Then we noticed their father, Mr. Barron, coming from the other direction. Papa headed for him at a fast clip. When the men met, we could hear every word between them: "Mista Harry," he said, "ah don't like ya whippin' my boys."

"Your boys are working for me," Papa said, "and anyone who is supposed to be working for me is going to work. You know that. I whipped my boys and I whipped yours. I'm sorry about that — but they have to learn to work."

"Yas, suh, Mista Harry," he agreed.

For the remainder of the day, our hoes were only blurs as we were somehow inspired to become consummate cotton choppers.

Edell said, "I even carried the water faster after seeing what happened. When Papa told us what to do he would tell us one time. If we didn't obey, we knew what to expect." That type of consistency is what many believe is needed today.

The boys learned to work hard and to stay with it until the job was done. Papa insisted that the job be done properly and completed on time. Halfway jobs raised Papa's ire and almost raised the poor performer off the ground when Papa's belt was applied. Lester learned to do all things well. He was a good athlete, speaker, worker, student, husband, father, evangelist, pastor, fisherman, and hunter.

5

Labors and Rewards

Picking cotton was hard work. Cotton-picking time in Texas falls in the hottest weeks of the year. Those days were remembered by the boys as torturous. These were the toughest days of their youth. The work was fast-paced. The pickers removed the fluffy cotton (containing the seeds) by hand and put it into large, unbleached canvas sacks they dragged behind them. The burrs on the dried bolls that held the cotton were sharp. In picking, fiber and seeds were grasped between the thumb and the fingers and pulled out of the dry boll. It was impossible to do this as quickly as was necessary without occasionally grasping a sharp burr; this was painful until the fingers were toughened. Cotton was picked from every boll, and since the cotton plants were quite short, the picker had to stoop or work from a kneeling position. Trying to pick cotton while kneeling relieved the back but was painful without leather knee pads. This method also made it difficult to drag the heavy sack of cotton. Most good cotton pickers worked primarily from the stooping position.

"Lester was the best cotton picker in the family." Melvin said.

Melvin was the record keeper or *weigher*. He met each worker as he came to the wagon to weigh and empty the cotton from his sack into the wagon. When Lester came to the wagon to weigh out, he placed the shoulder strap of his sack on the scale hook and then used a rope from the same hook to go under the middle of the long sack full of cotton. When the other end of the rope was tied to the scale hook and cinched up tight, it pulled the entire sack of cotton up and clear of the ground. It was then totally suspended from the hook on the cotton scale. Melvin moved the pea along the beam of the scale until it balanced in the horizontal position. Behind that pea shank, the weight was read from the numbers imprinted on the scale beam. He carefully read the weight. Then Melvin entered the amount in the record book beside Lester's name. The same procedure was used as Edell, Homer, Buddy, Sunno, and the other workers pulled their heavy sacks to the wagon to be weighed.

Since Melvin was the *weigher*, he picked less cotton than Edell or Lester. When the wagon was full, Papa came with a team of mules and hooked them to the wagon. Then, with the reins in hand, he climbed onto the wagon; sitting on the piled-high cotton, he shouted, *"Giddyup!"* The mules strained against the trace chains, and the heavy wagon began to move slowly as the wooden-spoked, steel-rimmed wheels sank into the soft black soil. The pulling was made easier when the hard-packed turn-row was reached.

The excitement of having a load of long-awaited cotton on the wagon usually made the trip to the gin enjoyable. This is a special time in a cotton farmer's life; there is a sense of accomplishment that is rarely equaled in other vocations. Edell was the only one of the boys who later sensed that satisfaction. He was successful in the farming business for forty-four years.

After the grueling day the boys were always glad to get back to the old farmhouse. After supper Papa sat with the boys in the breeze on the back porch. Papa asked, "Boys, how much cotton did you pick today?"

Each of us would report how much cotton we picked. Lester's report was always the best.

"Boys," Papa said with obvious pride, "you picked almost a bale of cotton today. You are getting to be good cotton pickers."

Melvin said, "Papa was a man of few words. He didn't make long flowery speeches, but we were just as proud as if he had. We knew we had met his expectation — that was all that counted."

Melvin described what Saturdays were like during cotton-picking time:

Papa was quick to commend us when we did a good job; that was our reward. But, during cotton-picking season, we received extra compensation in the form of pocket change. The usual nickel or dime was increased to fifty cents. We could spend it on Saturdays when we all went to Dawson; that was a lot of money to blow in one-day's time. An ice cream cone cost a nickel; a hamburger at Ponder's Hamburger Stand cost a dime — or three-for-a-quarter. During cotton picking season we had more money than most of the other boys in town.

Usually, we ran into Grandpa on Main Street. "How you boys doing? — now you just hold on a minute," he said without waiting for a reply. "Maybe your grandpa can find a dime for you." He got his leather change pouch out of his pocket; it was about six inches long and had a shiny metal snap to keep the hinged opener closed. He opened it and ceremoniously dug around inside. There was no doubt that he had the dimes because he had it all planned to give each of his grandsons a dime every Saturday. "Ah," he said as he found one, "here is a dime for you, Sonny Boy. Now you have a good time." He did the same for Edell and Lester. After we received our dimes from him, we each had sixty cents. We might have been a little cocky about our fortunes.

I usually took one of my friends (we will call him Luther, but that wasn't his name) into Matthew's Drugstore; I walked up to the counter and said, "Give me two large root beers — one for me and one for Luther here." I was so rich I could afford to be magnanimous in my generosity. Luther's parents couldn't afford to give him any money to spend.

One Saturday, Luther made a request that humbled me a little. He looked at the floor and said, "Melvin, will you let me have a dime so I can order the root beers today?"

"Sure, Luther," I said while digging in my overall's right front pocket. "Here is the dime."

Luther went up to the counter, walking as tall as possible. "Give me two large root beers," he said, as nonchalantly as he could manage, "one for me and one for Melvin here." He looked so pleased when he handed me the root beer. I know he wasn't nearly as pleased as I was, and I am still getting such pleasure from that memory; I wish I had done a lot more things like that.

Those long, hot rows in the cotton fields were somehow made just a bit shorter by their anticipation of Papa's praise and Saturday's celebration.

6

The Hunter

Someone said, "You can tell a lot about a man when he is hunting." Brother Roloff was a dead-eye with a shotgun. Watching him hunt quail was thrilling.

One day near Mission, Texas, we went out among the Ruby Red grapefruit groves. A large abandoned citrus grove which had been cleared of trees was our destination. We drove along the caliche road raising a cloud of dust. "It's a good thing this car is white," he said, "the white dust from the caliche doesn't show up so much."

It was a hot day; the sky was azure blue. We admired the large golden yellow grapefruit having only a blush of pink, hanging in striking contrast to the dark green tree foliage. The temptation was to abandon the hunt and enjoy the tree-ripened, ruby-red fruit.

When we arrived where we were to hunt, we were only three miles from the ministry's Peaceful Valley Home for older Christians. Brother Roloff stopped the car, and the show began. He got his gun out of the back seat of the Chevrolet. When the trunk was opened, two beautiful brown and white bird dogs jumped out. "What a different world it would be if people went about their jobs like these dogs," he said. The dogs stood trembling. "Wait a minute," they were admonished. He loaded the automatic 12 gauge Winchester and started walking toward the level field which was covered with dead, brown, Johnson grass, standing about knee-high. When the dogs saw the direction he was going, they could not contain themselves. They moved quickly ahead, not bounding and jumping as untrained pets might do. They stayed on the ground, noses down, running quietly. Within one minute one dog was on a picture-perfect point: her tail pointed straight back, the right front leg straight forward with the paw pulled sharply back. Not a muscle moved; her large eyes were fixed on a covey of quail. We slowly worked our way within shooting distance, the flush command was given, and the dog lunged toward the covey. Three birds flew with their customary and sometimes startling flutter. As usual, they split into an ever-widening pattern. When they were at a safe height for shooting, Brother Roloff let loose with three shots in rapid succession. Three birds fell. The dog was joined by her mate to find the dead birds, and quickly two birds were transported loosely in the dogs' mouths to their master. One bird was not found. The dogs spread out and began hunting again. "Dead bird," shouted Brother Roloff. Immediately the two dogs returned to look for the bird. Shortly, the third quail was retrieved. This was repeated until the limit was reached. Since the dogs had no understanding of limits, they wanted to continue hunting. When the trunk of the car was opened, they hesitated and looked up with droopy, sad eyes, but at the first command, in they jumped.

Harry Roloff had a conviction that his boys should be experts at anything they did. They were to be competitive and winners. He believed if they worked hard, fast, and expertly on the farm, they would do the same in any chosen vocation and would make a positive contribution to society. He decided he would not fail his boys by allowing them to do just the things they wanted to do, or to do things their own way, at their own speed. He knew good followers make good leaders. That conviction of Papa's was paramount in molding Lester to be an incessant campaigner for obedience, hard work, and superior performance in every undertaking.

7

Tempering Toughness with Tenderness

Was Papa respected just because he demanded things from his boys in terms that could not be misunderstood? Melvin tells a story that shows another side of Papa Roloff.

Early one morning I was with Lester and Edell out by the barn. Lester began mimicking the way Papa had given us our orders for the day. Lester could sound just like Papa with very little changing of his voice.

"You boys," he said, "I want you to chop the cotton over in the north forty acres today. I don't want any playing around, and if you know what's good for you, you will finish that job today. Do you understand what I am telling you?" To our amusement, Lester very graphically described the harsh punishment that would be inflicted on us if the orders were not obeyed. He said things like, "Your britches won't hold shucks." Everything was exaggerated and in the stern sounding voice of our father.

What Lester did not know was that Papa had come around the corner of the barn and was about ten feet behind him listening to every word he was saying. Edell and I knew Lester was in deep trouble. Lester sensed that everything was not exactly right when the grins on our faces suddenly turned to grimaces. Lester slowly turned around to find himself looking eye-to-eye into the Mount Rushmore-like face of our father, Mr. Harry Roloff. There was a moment of dead silence (Lester was praying quite intently — if he had good sense). That short moment afforded us all the time needed for our eardrums to do a "tom-tom" sounding heart rate analysis. Then, to the surprise of all of us, our father burst out laughing. Lester seemed stunned for a moment; then he made an effort to laugh. A little refrain of *huh-huh*s came out that were in stark discord with the lingering look of terror on his face. When Edell and I began laughing big time (we were not on the hot seat), Lester changed his mock amusement into a laughter of great relief. The entire scene was hilarious. Then Lester got an "I-made-a-funny" smirk on his face. We could hardly get our breath, and the chickens were frightened by the unusual, convulsive cackling that filled the barnyard that morning.

They were not at all cognizant of the fact that this Papa and sons' team had just taken a giant step of love toward one another. Papa's variable temperament of being stern and alternately being tender was to be remembered and practiced often by Lester in the years to come.

That scene was not planned — if it had been, it would have been forgotten quickly. They looked back on it with fond memories. The spoken reassurance of love from their father was remembered less than his actions because some things are indeed better *"felt than telt."*

These qualities of Harry Roloff were contagious. Lester developed the same closeness with many boys and girls who were in the Roloff Homes.

Champ was a ten-year-old black boy, but he was already in trouble with the law when he was sent to the ministry's

Lighthouse Home for Boys. The "Lighthouse," as it was called, was located on Padre Island. Built on the banks of the Intracoastal Canal, it was forty miles south of Corpus Christi, Texas, and bordered by the gigantic and famous King Ranch on one side and the sand dunes of the island on the other. The winds from the Gulf of Mexico tempered the hot summer days but made the winter cold spells almost unbearable.

When Brother Roloff was visiting there, he made it a practice to set aside part of the afternoon for his personal quiet time for Bible memorization and prayer. He enjoyed getting by himself at the peacefully-quiet guest cabin which was back near the sand dunes and separated from the barracks, dining facilities, boat docks, and piers.

One afternoon he was taking a watermelon to the guest cabin when Champ saw him. "Oh, Brother Roloff," he said excitedly as he came running, "are you going to eat that watermelon?"

"Why yes, Champ, that is exactly what I had in mind," he replied.

"Are you going to eat all of it?" asked Champ.

"That is my plan," said Brother Roloff.

"I like watermelon," the young boy said.

"Well, Champ, there will be all the watermelon you can eat tonight," the preacher reasoned.

"That's an awful long time from now," Champ said timidly.

Brother Roloff forced a frown as he looked down into the large white eyes and ebony face of this little boy who had a long-as-he-was-tall record of stealing from anyone whatever he wanted. Brother Roloff thought, *This lovable little boy has even stolen my heart.* Papa's alternating temperament began to take control. "Really, Champ, this watermelon is for me . . . and a fine little boy named Champ," he said with a broad smile. "Come on, sonny boy, let's hurry and get with it."

What a touching scene, Brother Roloff holding the watermelon in one arm, and the other arm around Champ's small shoulders as the barefooted pair walked down the deep, white sand path to the guest cabin.

Not every worker could get the cooperation and trust from the youths in the homes with the success that Brother Roloff enjoyed. The obvious reason was the unforced, genuine concern that radiated from a God-given, brimful heart of love. Whatever is in the heart will come out, and rebellious youths have a way of putting it to the test. Many people who tried to work at the Roloff Homes were astounded at their own fleshly reactions to provocations from youngsters who were there to be helped and to be trained by Christian example.

A tenderness in Brother Roloff was manifested in so many ways and with such consistency that it drew the children to him like a magnet.

Melvin relates an incident that happened while they were growing up on the farm. It has become a classic and speaks eloquently of the tender atmosphere in the Roloff home. He calls it the story of "Old Jesse."

Eight mules on the farm pulled the wagons, cultivators, planters, plows, and other farm implements. As these mules grew old, Papa traded them for younger mules that would be stronger for the long days of pulling heavy loads.

There was one special mule we called Jesse. We got him in 1910. He was a large, black mule and stronger than the other mules; he was the hardest worker on the farm.

One Friday the "mule trader" was in Dawson with

dozens of good-looking, young, healthy, Missouri mules. Papa decided that it was time to trade. He took the mules into town to see what kind of deal he could make with the trader.

Late that afternoon Papa came back to the farm with all new mules. He put them in the pen and leaned on the fence rail admiring the animals and relishing his good fortune.

It was time to wash up for supper; Papa went to the house. When he came up on the back porch and opened the screen door, Mama was waiting.

"Harry," she said, "did you get the new mules?"

"Yes, and I got some of the best looking Missouri mules in the country."

"Harry, you didn't trade off old Jesse did you?" she asked.

"Sure did," Papa replied, "and I made the best trade I've ever made. We have the best looking mules I've ever seen."

"Harry, you shouldn't have traded off old Jesse; he helped make every dollar you ever made on this farm," she admonished. "He was the best mule you ever had."

"Yes, he was a good mule all right — is supper ready?"

Papa spent most of the weekend working on the mules with a curry comb. They were shining so that he could almost see his reflection in their sides.

Not much was said, and everyone seemed content to be alone with his own thoughts. Those thoughts were mostly about losing old Jesse.

Early Monday morning Papa hooked up a team of mules to the wagon and announced that he was going to Dawson.

"Why are you going to Dawson?" Mama asked.

"Sally," he answered with a question, "do I have to tell you what I'm going to do every time I go into town?"

"No, I guess not," Mama said hesitantly.

Monday afternoon Papa came driving the wagon into the yard. Plodding along behind the wagon was old Jesse. Everyone ran out to meet them. No one asked questions. We all took turns hugging old Jesse's neck while Mama dabbed at her tears and the boys tried to hide their own — Papa was beaming.

When thinking back on this scene, Lester would probably agree with the saying: "The whole is greater than the sum of its parts." He thought, *The tender reunion of the family far outweighed the mistakes and the hurting that led to it.*

Edell explained further, "Mama had a special interest in Jesse because she used him when she plowed. She always used Jesse and Rodie."

Jesse was never traded again. He worked several more years and could still *outpull* every mule on the place. As Jesse got older, his black hair started turning gray until there was no more black. In retirement, his hair started turning white. Finally, Jesse was snow white. His death was mourned by the family. Another mule never took his place in their hearts; he almost seemed part of the family.

Brother Roloff was understandably a tenderhearted leader; he learned from his father to use everything, even his mistakes, to touch hearts and heal relationships.

He also had his father's ability to become very stern when it was necessary. His way of confronting a rebellious youth or worker was surely a gift from God because of its effectiveness. He could be very stern; the next minute he might be very tender. There was something about the alternating approach that could break through the toughest shell, one that was impenetrable by a direct unchanging approach. Many hard and bitter youths were disarmed by this alternating temperament. The Roloffs could trace the method to the book of Proverbs and Christ's New Testament instructions to fathers.

8

Playing for Keeps

Brother Roloff attributed much to the little one-room school named "Headquarters School," which he and his brothers attended. It was located on the property just north of their farm. His brother Melvin, who is a successful businessman in Victoria, Texas, believes it is the most effective way of teaching youngsters. Headquarters School had eight grades taught in that one room. All of the students were there no matter which grade was being taught. He said he attended the eighth grade seven times (he skipped one grade).

Melvin considered his a very good education. When he transferred to "town" school for his high school years, he immediately began making all *A's*. When asked for an explanation, he stated, "There was not much going on back in Headquarters School; there was nothing to keep us from learning as lessons were taught, even those meant for a higher level group. We could learn extremely well if we would just listen."

There were sins and temptations that came with student associations. Papa and Mama Roloff seemed to put the avoidance of these sins and temptations at a high level in their priorities. They addressed most of them before they were actually faced by the boys.

Brother Roloff told the following story:

Many years ago when I was a little boy living in

Navarro County, about five miles from Dawson, Texas, I became the king of marble shooters. It was a great game; we spent many hours shooting marbles. We had a game we called "Puggy" that had three holes in the dirt; it became quite a science. There was another game we called "Playing for Keeps" which was considered gambling, at least by my mother, and I am sure she was right. We would put our marbles in a ring on the ground; the one who shot them out got to keep them so we called it "Playing for Keeps."

My mother said to me, "Lester, you must never play for keeps, because that's gambling." I agreed with her and promised her faithfully that I would not. I managed not to, though I knew I could have won anybody's marbles because of my expert marble shooting ability. The sound exhortation and warning from my mother protected me — until one day down at the bottom of the school ground.

I had very few marbles, maybe some old steel balls and an old cracked marble or two. Frank, a boy who came to our school, was the son of a big landowner. He had every color marble in the rainbow — all kinds and all colors. There was a marble called an agate that every marble shooter admired and wanted. Frank had an agate; there seemed to be no end to his marbles.

One day Frank said, "Lester, I'll shoot you some *Keeps*." The glitter and my lust and desire to have some nice marbles overcame my mother's warning.

I said quickly, "Put them in the ring," and we started shooting marbles for keeps. Of course I shot every marble he had out of the ring and put them in my pocket.

Finally, he said, "Stake me one on my taw." (Now the taw was the one we shot with, which means that was his last marble.) I put one in the ring for him and shot it out; I got every marble he had. My pockets were full of marbles. It was time to go back to class after the lunch period. We ran and got in line; we always lined up and marched in and marched out.

From lunch time until the afternoon recess there came a struggle and a disturbance inside of me as I sat at the old-fashioned school desk. I thought, *The first question is what will my explanation be when I get home with all these beautiful marbles?* And of course the devil suggested: *I could hide them under the house and take them out a few at a time to play with them.* But that didn't settle the disturbance. I sat at my desk, and I thought I heard my mother say, *Son, you're not going to play marbles for keeps, that's gambling.* And I heard myself say, *No, Ma'am, I'm not going to be a gambler.* As a little boy God had given me conviction, and the battle was raging on the inside. I almost felt like I had turned into a professional gambler. But then the devil said, *Frank is well able to buy himself plenty of marbles. And, after all, you won them because you were the best shot. And you deserve them because of your ability, and he was the one who asked you to shoot marbles for keeps.* None of that seemed to give me peace or satisfaction.

When recess came, the teacher asked me to stay in for one reason or another. I sat at my desk and was the only one in the room when the door opened; Frank came walking in and said, "Lester, would you loan me a marble for a shooting taw?"

It was then I said, "Hold out both hands." I poured all the marbles out of my book sack into his hands.

He said, "I just wanted one because the rest of them belong to you."

"I don't want any of them," I said, "except my old marbles that I had." I picked my marbles out and put them in my pocket, and I doubt if I've ever been bigger or felt better before that time or since. I'd given back the same thing as stolen marbles.

All of the other temptations were handled in the same manner as "Playing for Keeps." When an occasion arose, their mama or papa looked the boys directly in the face and said solemnly, "You know better'n that." That settled it. The boys loved their parents and did not want to do anything to hurt them. They knew their parents loved them and only told them the truth.

The playing-for-keeps story does not end with Lester giving the marbles back to Frank. There was a direct confirmation that God honored that conviction on gambling in later years. Brother Roloff continues:

Many years later I was asked to bring my revival tent to my hometown in Dawson, Texas, set it up on Main Street, and preach a revival. What a glorious time that was. My dad and the people who worked for him helped put up the tent. The revival started, and lifelong friends and neighbors came to the meeting. I noticed a fine looking man in the audience whose name was Frank, the one who had had all the nice marbles. He was not a Christian. Saturday night, just before the meeting closed, I went back to him during the invitation and told him I'd been praying for him ever since the Lord called me to preach and that I wanted him to be saved. He went to the altar with me and gave his heart to Christ. He asked me to baptize him, which I was happy to do. The experience was worth more than all the marbles in the world put together. . . . The Bible says, "Provide things honest in the sight of all men." And, "Whatsoever things are true, whatsoever things are honest, whatsoever things are just, whatsoever things are pure, whatsoever things are lovely, whatsoever things are of good report; if there be any virtue, and if there be any praise, think on these things" (Phil. 4:8).

Frank knew gambling was wrong. If Lester had not given his marbles back to him, Frank possibly would have seen him as a hypocrite and used that as a reason not to attend the revival meeting. There is no doubt God honors those who hold Bible principles high — especially those who yield to them as youths. They then become part of the very infrastructure of their character that will not be destroyed later by the shifting winds of an indulgent and licentious society.

9

Singing Lessons

Melvin confides, "The only thing we ever learned about singing, Mama taught us. She was always singing. We woke up in the morning to her singing. Two songs I can remember her singing while she cooked breakfast were 'In the Sweet By and By' and 'Down by the Riverside.' I can hear her now," he said. "She wasn't much of a singer, but look how we remember! Of all the good things about Mama, that's what I remember the most."

Edell remembers hearing his mother sing "The Old Rugged Cross" and "Rock of Ages." He said, "Finally we got an old used piano. Mama could play it, and we would have the church people over for singing after the evening services. The only songs we sang were gospel songs. We all remember the good times we had singing around that piano."

Lester caught the singing spirit from his mother. He sang no matter what his location or who was listening. Gene Price was "turned off" by Brother Roloff's singing and preaching. But it was through the singing of that "harsh voice," he said, "breaking all the laws of rhythm, . . . the message of the song was coming through — right into my heart." After Gene became a Christian, he and Francis were married, and he joined with her in serving the Lord.

Brother Roloff's older daughter, Elizabeth Ann, saw her father as the "best singer, whistler, story teller, preacher, father, and the best just about everything."

The Family Altar Program has as a closing theme song "The Stranger by the Sea," which is always sung by Brother Roloff. This is not a well-known song and is rarely used in church services. One day Brother Roloff was traveling in another city, and he walked into a rest room. Inside, a Latin American boy was singing *They came and they were blessed, He gave the weary rest, He made the blinded eyes to see. . . .* Brother Roloff said to the boy, "Hey, what are you doing singing my song?"

The boy looked up at him and asked hesitantly, "Are you *Father* Roloff?"

He was criticized as a singer, and he was loved as a singer. Most people agreed, however, that his songs always had a wonderful, Christ-honoring, and Bible-based message. All of the singing groups from the homes sang songs based on that same criteria.

Some of these groups were the most melodious singers anywhere. Then there were some who didn't have much to offer other than the lyrics. "What a rag-tag bunch of singers that was," was heard after a service. Then they added, "But when you consider where they came from, it was heavenly." Somehow, Brother Roloff's preaching and the group's singing belonged together. He once commented after a tour through the South, "We have finally arrived."

"What do you mean?" someone asked.

"We held a service with our singing group in the Bob Jones University Amphitorium," he replied. Being a man of God who had the strength of his convictions served to open many wonderful doors of service.

Once he reported from his pulpit that he would never sing publicly again. The audience was silent. He continued, "Someone asked me, 'Why do you sing in the services? You sound just like someone hollerin' in a rain barrel.'" The crowd roared, and he laughed with them — then he sang a song — make that two songs.

His office workers said he was an incessant singer and whistler.

Over the years, mail from radio listeners begged him to sing more, less, or not at all.

His mama had a song in her heart she could not contain. Her youngest son's all-round circumstances seemed more under control than they often were because his mama taught him to *just keep on praying (and singing) till the light breaks through.*

Much is learned about this man's theology by the messages of the songs he sang. They tell the story of his life and the lives of many Christians. Even the song titles give the message and describe his burden. The following little story uses only the titles of songs included in the 1994 cassette of Brother Roloff, "Singing from the Heart." The cassette was made to celebrate fifty years of broadcasting the Family Altar Program. There was a great demand for the tape (RO 2050). Notice the *song titles* give the gospel message.

Deeper Than the Stain

God leads us along till the storm passes by. Hold on a little longer listening at the heart's door — call unto Me. God will take care of you. Constantly abiding, He's the keeper of my soul; no one ever cared for me like Jesus. Just keep on praying; keep in touch with Jesus. Remembering, in Heaven He the pearly gates will open. He bore the cross for me. I would not be denied the blood that stained the old rugged cross.

Himself

Then Jesus came — the stranger by the sea. I am so glad He giveth more grace — He is so precious to me. Jesus whispers peace in my heart in the shelter of His arms. Come and dine in the garden with Jesus.

There were others around the Roloff farm who were singers. The boys held make-believe church services. Sometimes Lester sang. Sunno also sang, and he believed in singing for all he was worth — and in three parts. Later, Lester imitated how Sunno sang in three parts. He sang with gusto:

Life's evening sun, life's evening sun, life's evening sun,

Is sinking low, is sinking low, is sinking low,

A few more days, a few more days, a few more days,

And I must go, and I must go, and I must go. . . .

After the singing there was preaching. Lester was usually chosen to preach because he remembered the exhortations of the evangelists who occasionally preached in the Shiloh and Harmony churches. One day Lester actually baptized an old hen (chicken variety). He plunged her into a barrel of water and then set her on the ground; as the soaked and terrified chicken moved out with all available speed — half running and half flying — Lester said, "Bless you, my sister." To some this might border on being sacrilegious, but, remember, most of what these boys knew about life and playing like adults centered around the church.

He often longed for the friends and security of that isolated farm, but he knew those days were gone. Those blissful days were days of preparation, fixing priorities, building character, and the bending of the twig. *My parents did their part,* he reminded himself, *and I'll not let God and my godly parents down. I'll stand for Him and His Word as long as He gives me breath.*

10

The Burden

Lamp for the feet that in byways have wandered,
Guide for the youth that would otherwise fall:
Hope for the sinner whose life has been squandered,
Staff for the aged, and best Book of all.

— Anon.

Was helping the helpless something Brother Roloff just
happened upon after trying other things? Many will be
surprised to learn that the City of Refuge was not the first
home he started for alcoholics. One was started during his
pastorate at Trinidad, Texas, while he was still in the
seminary.

Several hundred acres were set aside by a ranch owner
for Lester to start the work. The property was near the little
Central Texas town of Buda. The work began, and the
alcoholics started coming; small cabins were built to provide decent living quarters. The preacher came as often as
possible from Trinidad, where he was the pastor of a
growing Baptist church.

Lester's brother Melvin enjoys telling the story of an
alcoholic barber from Detroit, Michigan, who was brought
to the home.

One night someone brought in a man who was so
drunk he didn't know his own name. The next day,
when the preacher arrived, the man was sober. When

introduced to Lester, the man said, "Preacher, I don't even know what I'm doing here. I don't know who brought me. I haven't been sober in the last twelve years. But since I'm here, if there is any way you can help me, I sure would appreciate it."

Lester said, "Only One can help you, and His name is Jesus Christ, and He loves you."

"*Aw*, Preacher," the man said, "no one can love a man as sorry as I am. You don't know some things I have done and how many people I have hurt and cheated. Alcohol helps keep my mind dull to all those things."

"I don't know the things you have done," Lester said, "but Jesus knows all about you, and He is willing to forgive you from all those past sins. He is also willing to change your heart so you will not act that way in the future."

"But, Preacher, I am nothing but a sot; I would never be able to stay away from my booze. I have a wife and two sons up in Detroit who won't have anything to do with me. You know, no one in the whole world loves me."

"You are possibly right, but we love you because we have His love in our hearts," Lester said. "He loved you enough to take your guilt on Himself. Your own sins were included in the sins that were laid on Him when He was crucified on a Roman cross near Jerusalem, on a hill called Mount Calvary. 'But God commendeth His love toward us, in that, while we were yet sinners, Christ died for us.' You can stay here, and we can help you if you will listen to what we teach. God is willing and able to help you."

After about six weeks the man said, "Brother Roloff, I want to help any way I can while I am here. I am a barber; if there is any way we can fix up a little barbershop, I will take care of all the haircutting."

"That is a spirit I like; I will do the best I can to get some equipment," Lester said.

The word was spread. About two weeks later a truck arrived with a good used barber's chair that someone had donated. There were electricians, plumbers, and carpenters in the home for help. They pitched in, and soon there was a fairly well equipped barber's shop. It had plumbing, electricity, large mirrors on the freshly painted walls, and the used barber's chair.

The barber worked faithfully for nearly six months. Then one day when Brother Roloff drove up to the home, the barber was waiting for him with his white barber's shirt on and an envelope in his hand.

"Brother Roloff," he said seriously, "I have a letter here from my wife; she and my two boys want me to come home. I have not had a drink for over six months, and I think I can make it with God's help. Would you let me go home to Mama and the boys? They say they miss me something awful. It's been ten years, and I want to show them what has happened to Daddy."

"O.K.," Lester smiled. "If you promise me you will attend a good Bible-believing church and take your family with you, I will let you go. But you must remember to read your Bible with your family every day and pray with them."

"I will buy a bus ticket for you and give you a sack lunch. I will not give you any money because I don't want you tempted along the way."

Several weeks passed. Then Brother Roloff received a letter. It was written by the barber's wife. "Oh, Brother Roloff, how can we thank you for Daddy? He is here, and we are enjoying him so much. The boys were only babies when he left, but now you should see how he is playing with them and teaching them Christian principles. They love him so much. We are the happiest family in the world. Daddy has his old job back at the barbershop, and the men there can't stop talking about the change in him. He tells them Jesus did it all."

"We are attending a good church, and we are having our own family altar. We are sending this money to help in the work. We will send more as we have it." (A ten-dollar bill was enclosed.)

"Please don't ever stop what you are doing."

He never stopped. The Alameda Baptist Church in Corpus Christi, Texas, assumed the responsibility of the local Good Samaritan Rescue Mission while Brother Roloff was the pastor there. He also started a Good Samaritan Rescue Mission in Big Spring, Texas. All of these ministries were before the "first" City of Refuge in Lee County, Texas, near Lexington. It is clear the burden for fallen people was not a Johnny-come-lately impulse in his ministry.

It was not that he specialized in the poor and the *down-and-outers*; his ministry was open to all. It seemed that people didn't seek help until they hit the bottom. The homes were (and are) open to any race, social level, religion, or creed.

Part Two

Lester Roloff — Living By Faith
Marie Brady Roloff

11

Dauntless Faith

It is rare indeed to find a man who is determined to live by his convictions. I married such a man. Not only did my husband, Lester Roloff, live by his convictions, but he lived by faith. The two, of course, are closely intertwined — they colored his personality, his prayer life, and his preaching; they influenced his entire life.

Standing up for his convictions at one point in his ministerial career cost Lester the favor of one of the largest denominations in this country. Yes, that hurt. As his wife, I understandably suffered right along with him. In the process of standing up for his convictions he founded churches, Christian schools, and the Roloff Evangelistic Enterprises, Inc., a nonprofit organization formed in 1951 which developed and supported many projects of faith. (That organization continues today and operates with the same objectives for which Lester Roloff lived and died.)

Lester's influence was and is far-reaching. Because of the

way God used him, there are hundreds of men and women in full-time Christian service around the world and thousands of Christian laymen and laywomen, teen-agers, and boys and girls who have come into a vital relationship with Jesus Christ. In succeeding chapters I want to share with you what brought all of this about. I am thankful the Lord allowed me to be the wife of a man whose life touched so many others.

Through the pages of this book I want to take you to the City of Refuge in Culloden, Georgia, where on 273 acres there is a beautiful old antebellum home and some lovely dormitories that were used for housing alcoholics. That work has since been moved, along with all of the other works, into the large complex located at the church and farm near Corpus Christi, Texas. The work of snatching men from alcoholism continues to go on day after day. The stories coming out of the City of Refuge are miraculous.

We will walk together through the Peaceful Valley Home. This home was for Christians who were of retirement age. This was the home of prayer — much prayer — where these men and women could live and still be of service to others. It was their prayers that provided strong undergirding for the diverse work of the Roloff Evangelistic Enterprises.

You will be amazed at the Anchor Home for Boys in Zapata, Texas, where boys who had nowhere else to go were warmly welcomed, loved, and cared for. The home had a dormitory capacity of nearly three hundred, a cafeteria, a dining room, a gymnasium, and shop buildings.

The Bethesda Home for Girls in Hattiesburg, Mississippi, was for girls in trouble. Before birth-control pills and abortion were so common, the home took in pregnant, unwed girls.

Corpus Christi, Texas, is the location of the Rebekah Home for Girls. This home opened in 1967. This is the same time the People's Church was started. We have taken into the home several thousand girls, worked with them in their schooling and rehabilitation, and introduced them to the One who has the answers to life's complexities. There are three dorms with a combined capacity of about three hundred.

On the 465 acres of farmland near Corpus Christi, Texas, stands the Rebekah Home, the People's Church, the Christian school, a bakery, a vehicle maintenance shop, a tractor and implement building, a hospitality house, our home, an aircraft hanger and runway. There are also house trailers for the workers who are connected with the school, the shops, the farm, and the homes. Here too we have vegetable gardens, and cows and goats that supply milk for the homes.

Subsequent to the original printing of this book, the Lighthouse, the Anchor Home, the City of Refuge, and the Jubilee Home were also constructed on this acreage.

Lester stood firm in his convictions in the controversy with the state of Texas. As a result, he spent time in jail; he was brought before nine judges of the Texas Supreme Court; he was engaged with the Texas Welfare Department in a battle that cost great sums of money. My husband's name has been maliciously slandered. But the greatest cost in all this was the heartache and harassment he endured at the hands of those who violated the first amendment to the Constitution. This amendment was to protect the church from state controls. All those who were supportive of the work and the young people who had to be turned out of the homes suffered with Lester in his heartache. The battle is not over. We pray that God will see to it that many of the fallen youths of America will again be salvaged by these great and unique homes, and that Christian churches will be free again.

We will tell you of the old Lighthouse for Boys which was forty miles down the Intracoastal Canal from Corpus Christi and was accessible only by boat or plane. Living here were young men who had been imprisoned for various crimes — they were actually society's incorrigibles. Here, as in the other projects, my husband's unshakable faith and his strong convictions always played a major role.

Another vital phase of the Roloff Evangelistic Enterprises' ministry is the Family Altar Broadcast. It began in 1944 on a local 250-watt radio station and at its zenith was on 160 radio stations across the nation, as well as in the Virgin Islands, the West Indies, Alaska, and Hawaii. Daily devotional cassette tapes of messages by Lester are sent out regularly in response to the mail requests from nearly 100 stations that continue to air the program.

Living for his convictions was a costly venture for this dynamo of a man. This is not uncommon, however, for men and women in the forefront of the action. The pages of history — both secular and biblical — bear this out. A look at Hebrews 11, that great "roll-call-of-faith" chapter in the Bible, illustrates clearly the fact that the history of the nation of Israel and the early church was written by faith, often at the cost of the saints' blood.

The biographies of men and women of past centuries reveal Christian heroism that we know very little of today. Flesh-and-blood people suffered and triumphed in other generations. One can scarcely imagine the dangers, hardships, and trials they were called upon to endure. I think of Adoniram and Ann Judson, who cast their lot among barbarians in Burma; and Mary and Robert Moffat, who bore with unflinching calm and good temper the perils, discomforts, and discord of travel into the interior of uncharted Africa to spend their lives in savage surroundings. So many others come to mind — John Williams and his wife Mary, who labored tirelessly among the natives of the South Sea Islands; and William Tyndale, who translated the Bible into English and paved the way for the King James Version of the Bible. Tyndale was tried for treason and heresy against the church. He was condemned and strangled, and his body was burned.

All of these people valued the gospel more than their lives and were prepared to stand for what they believed even if it meant death. Their faith was dauntless.

I don't feel it is an exaggeration to say that these early contenders for the faith had a modern counterpart in the man I married. It is almost unthinkable today in this country that a man should be willing to go to jail for his convictions, but go to jail he did, and more than once.

It is not surprising that the Texas newspapers have depicted Lester Roloff as a combination Elmer Gantry and Marjoe who went around "whippin' little girls for God." The media have questioned the way our Enterprises are supported financially, and they have poked fun at Lester's radio broadcasts and his manner of preaching.

In this country we don't burn men at the stake for holding to their convictions. We are not cannibalistic so we do not eat our enemies. But civilized man has found other ways to punish those who run counter to ungodly bureaucratic edicts and unconstitutional laws; they are subjected to persecution and judgement that gnaw at the heart of a man who is innocent of ill intent.

I often muse about the years since our marriage in 1936. Certainly I knew Lester Roloff better than anyone else in the world. I lived with him longer than members of his own family, and he told me I was his best friend and, yes, his best critic, too. Certainly he had his shortcomings and imperfections, just as I do. The years together were rich years of learning. In the process we both learned much. In some ways I feel inadequate to write about this man even though I knew him so well.

More than one publication has stated that Lester Roloff was a complex man and that no one knew him well. He may have given that impression to others and even at times to those who knew him somewhat, but my husband was an open and honest individual. Perhaps it was this very thing — his honesty — that made him so vulnerable to criticism. By and large, the world was not accustomed to dealing with a man of principles and integrity. Lester did not plot against people nor engage in intrigue. He did not flatter; neither did he praise much. He was just what he seemed to be — a man of honor, a man who stood by his word.

Lester would have been the first to tell you, "Look, I'm just a sinner saved by grace — a Christian called to preach the Word of God." More than that, however, you will see that he was also a compassionate man.

12

And the Child Grew

There was a child went forth every day;
And the first object he look'd upon, that object he became;
And that object became part of him for the day, or a certain part of the day, or for many years, or stretching cycle of years. . . .
These became part of that child who went forth every day, and who now goes, and will always go forth every day.[1]

His child world was small. Beyond the walls of the Texas farm home and the fields of cotton lay a big world. His eyes grew wide with wonder as he listened to his elders talk. Grandfather Roloff talked of his coming to this country from Germany because the national conscription had begun taking away the liberty of the young men. "I didn't want any part in such foolishness, and so I came here to seek a fortune and keep my liberty," Grandfather reminisced. The child named Lester looked around at the humble home of his grandparents as the old gentleman continued, "Fortune? Well, we do have a home and a farm. Liberty? That we surely have . . ." and he expounded on one of his favorite themes complete with appropriate gestures.

---

[1] Walt Whitman, *There was a Child Went Forth.*

Doubtless, Lester, my husband, inherited much of his tenacity of character from this stubborn German grandfather whose speech was often more picturesque than correct.

The dawning of the twentieth century brought new hopes, new desires, and new thoughts to the American people. Little did they know that during this century they would see automobiles produced en masse, jet planes, radar, two world wars, the wars in Korea and Vietnam, radio, television, microwave cooking, laser-beam surgery, the atomic bomb, and the Depression of the 1930's. These and a host of other things brought about unanticipated changes.

The Roloff family was like many others. They were always looking for better and happier times. Grandfather Roloff had immigrated to Wisconsin where he found a bride, and together they headed for the vast state of Texas. Their first son, Harry Augustus, was born on June 12, 1889, in Patterson, Texas. Two other children blessed this household in rapid succession.

When Harry grew to manhood, he met a girl from Oletha, Texas. Sadie Isabel McKenzie had come into the world on April 11, 1892. She was only sixteen when young Harry captured her heart. This young woman would become the mother of my husband. At one time she told me that when they married, their families donated to them a mattress, springs, headboard, and linen. With these modest beginnings they started housekeeping.

The first child born to them was a girl who lived for only two weeks and is listed in the family Bible as "Baby Roloff." While living at Patterson, their next two children were born—Melvin and Edell.

The year was 1914. The conflict had begun with the assassinations of the archduke of Austria-Hungary and his wife. There were many basic causes for the war—the growth of nationalism, the system of military alliances that created a balance of power, the competition for colonies and other territory, and the use of secret diplomacy. Lester's grandparents, his parents, uncles and aunts, and neighboring friends often sat around and discussed what was happening across the ocean, and Sadie Roloff worried about the kind of world into which she would be bringing their next child. The United States tried to remain neutral, but in 1917 it joined the Allies, hoping to "make the world safe for democracy."

On June 28, 1914, in a modest German-Scottish farm home near Dawson, Texas, a baby boy was born to Harry and Sadie Roloff. They named this baby Lester Leo. Today, those who are involved in his ministry call him "Brother Roloff."

More than four years after my husband's birth, on November 11, 1918, the armistice was signed. War is always costly, and World War I was no exception. about sixty-three of every one hundred servicemen who died came from the Allied Armed Forces. Civilian deaths totaled about five million; starvation, disease, and exposure accounted for about eighty percent of these deaths. The economic loss was more than $337 billion. The war-shattered countries suffered greatly. The Roloff family understandably felt great concern; after all, Grandfather was from Germany. Some of that concern and hatred for oppression and its effect on people must have rubbed off on the young impressionable lad.

Two years after Lester's birth a second girl was born. She did not live to her teens, however; and her death was one of the major tragedies in the home. The shadow of the war and the death of a much-loved sister were early influences on the life of this growing child.

Lester grew up in a religiously divided but still harmonious home. The churches in his community were built side by side. Each church had a half-time pastor. Every other Sunday services were held at "Harmony," the Methodist church. Every family in the community attended the services at Harmony regardless of their religious affiliation. The entire Roloff family attended Harmony with their father and paternal grandparents, who were Methodist. On alternating Sundays the family attended services with their Baptist mother at the Shiloh Baptist Church next door. Lester maintains that to his knowledge no arguments ever arose over Baptist or Methodist doctrines.

Sunday School was a must for children and adults alike. The children's class was called the "card class." Lessons were printed on cards with Bible pictures and Scripture verses.

And then there was the yearly revival time. Usually this occurred in the month of July after cotton picking was over. On one occasion, when Lester was about thirteen, at the close of a service the pastor invited all those who had just been saved to remain at the front of the auditorium to receive the "right hand of Christian fellowship." Lester, along with many others, went down the line shaking hands with the new converts. As the family was returning home, his father turned to him and said emphatically, "Son, don't you *ever* go down and shake hands with people like that again."

Lester thought about that for a moment, then asked, "Why, Papa?"

"Because you do not have a Christian hand, that's why," was the reply.

Lester looked at his hand critically and compared it with his brothers' hands. He could see no outward difference. *Why isn't my hand a Christian hand?* he wondered. *How does a person get a Christian hand?* he asked himself. But he asked no questions, and no further explanations were given since the theory at that time was that children should be seen and not heard.

Lester was an obedient child. He obeyed his father's command and did not extend the hand of fellowship to new Christians again until after he himself was saved almost a year later. His own conversion took place during a July revival meeting. "I felt the Lord calling me to be saved," he has been heard to say on many occasions. "But I was timid," he explains, "and didn't want to make a move toward the front by myself. Finally, the lady who taught us in the card class came to me, put her arm around me, and said, 'Lester, don't you want to be saved?' I said, 'Yes, ma'am,' and with that admission, made my way to the altar to give the preacher my hand."

My husband recalls that after the service, before the "Amen" was said, the choir sang a hymn as everyone came by to hug or shake hands with the new converts. "There was a universal hugging going on," he tells. "All my relatives and friends rejoiced that I and others had been saved that night." The practice in many churches today does not differ much from the events of the day my husband came into the family of God. Salvation is always cause for rejoicing!

On the way home from that service Lester finally understood what his father had meant the summer before about his not having a "Christian hand." Now his hands were Christian, and his heart rejoiced because he, too, had trusted in Christ as his personal Savior.

13

The Freckle-Faced Country Boy

With great gusto grandfather Roloff twisted the dials and adjusted the huge loudspeaker. What was this strange contraption? The country folk came from miles around to see for themselves. Grandfather's radio was the curiosity of the country, and he played the role of radio engineer with obvious relish! There was a moment of breathless silence as everyone waited, no one moving or shifting his eyes from the set. Suddenly there came a blast of sound, a loud squeal and squawk, and the program began.

My husband was among those who sat wide-eyed and filled with wonder, an interested Saturday night bystander, breathless and inquisitive. No one could possibly have known that one day Lester Roloff's voice would be carried by 160 radio stations across the United States, the Virgin Islands, and the West Indies, and that his would be an ever-growing ministry.

Grandfather Roloff was also the proud owner of a Model-T Ford. It provided some never-to-be-forgotten memories for family members. To this day Lester remembers a certain trip they made to West Texas. On a stop for gasoline he got out of the car and raced across the road to spend a nickel. When he came back, the car was gone. Frightened and crying, he started running down the road. Finally, after what seemed an eternity to Lester, the family missed him and came back for him. Lester never enjoyed being alone, and he had never felt more alone than when he ran down that dusty road trying to catch a Model-T racing along at thirty miles per hour!

There is a certain loneliness unique to the man or woman in a place of leadership and responsibility. A man can be alone in a crowd. My husband is no stranger to that kind of loneliness.

There is also the loneliness that comes when a person is running away from himself. We encounter that kind of loneliness in the young people who come to our homes from all parts of the country. They feel bewildered, lost, and alone in their misery, shame, and sadness. Sometimes they are alone in their rebellion against parents and the world. They try to mask their inner pain. They represent every class of society. They are frightened and without hope, running down "dusty roads" that lead nowhere. Lester Roloff remembers the feelings that filled him on that dusty road in Texas.

Southern children are taught good manners and respect for adults early in life. Papa set the example for his boys in manners. His car was a Model-T Ford with red casings and spokes. When Papa used to drive down the road, he'd pull off his black hat at each neighbor's house and say "How do?" to the ladies. It was never, "How do you do?" just, "How do?"

Papa was a Christian gentleman, and godly manners were taught in the home. He would ask the boys, "What did you say, son?" If they answered, "Uh-huh" or "Yes," Papa was quick to remind them to say, "Yes, sir." The last thing Papa and Mama said to their boys when they left home to go visit was, "Son, mind your manners." Papa firmly believed Scripture taught this in 1 Corinthians 15:33, where it says:

"Be not deceived: evil communications corrupt good manners." This was his watchword for his three boys. "I believe in clean speech, hard work, and clean living," he would say with a certain firmness that implied, *"Watch out if you don't comply!"*

My husband comes by his compassionate nature quite naturally. His parents were always on call to friends and neighbors at any time of the day or night. His mother would help with the arrival of someone's baby or help to comfort the sorrowing in time of death. There was only one doctor in a ten-mile radius of Dawson, so Mrs. Roloff was often needed in the role of midwife. It was simply a matter of living by the Bible precepts the Roloffs believed. Regardless of the inconvenience, they were available to family and friends. When one of the boys would question them about this, they would say, "The Bible says, 'They helped every one his neighbour; and every one said to his brother, Be of good courage' " (Isa. 41:6.)

It is not hard for me to understand the compelling force that sends my husband out on errands of love and missions of mercy regardless of the weather or the time of day or night. There have been times when elaborate birthday celebrations in his honor or other plans have had to be canceled because he had to get in his plane and fly off to see some judge concerning a boy about to be sentenced or to respond to a weeping mother's plea: "Oh, Brother Roloff, please come and get our daughter. . . ."

My husband knew the value of nickels and dimes. He would not misuse and squander money entrusted to the Roloff Enterprises any more than he would have robbed his much-loved papa of his hard-earned money. At one point, when the Texas Welfare Department was making it so difficult for our Enterprises' work, Lester wrote to the faithful supporters and radio listeners, saying:

> The Bible says, "Render unto Caesar the things that are Caesar's, and unto God the things that are God's", and that we have done for over forty-one years. We have paid our taxes. We have been upright citizens, built Christian homes, and taught our children to build Christian homes. We have rendered good citizens who were once alcoholics and dope addicts. We have sent parent-hating, Satan-worshiping, dope-taking, immoral boys and girls back into society as preachers and preachers' wives and faithful servants of the Lord. We have never taken a penny of tax money and yet we have saved the state at least fifty million dollars during these nearly thirty years. The only ray of hope we have seen in this dark overcast for six long months has been the faithfulness of our pastor friends, churches, and Christians who have said, "Who knows but what you have come to the kingdom for such a time as this? Be our Mordecai or Moses." Well, dear friends, I will have to have some Esthers and Joshuas."

Papa was known for being brusque with his sons. My husband has been criticized for some of his seemingly stern ways. Papa was a strict disciplinarian though he loved his children deeply. My husband has always treated the young people who come under his care with firm discipline. Papa's orders were meant to be obeyed; Lester Roloff's rules are to be enforced by those in charge of the Enterprises' homes. This means that the boys and girls, the young men and women, and any others who come for help are expected to be obedient.

But there was one overriding factor that made all the difference in the world to Lester as he was growing

73

up—Papa's orders were accompanied by pet names such as "Honey" and "Sweetheart," even when his boys were full grown. The strictest command usually ended with the name "Honey." That may sound strange, but Papa was an unusual man. Likewise, Lester Roloff's disciplinary measures, although firm, are given with love. The people he deals with know it, and this accounts for the responsiveness, even from those who are considered the toughest, the most unruly, and the most unlikely to change.

We have many letters from young men and women who have stayed in one of the homes. One such letter spoke of the kind of love that the world finds so difficult to understand and accept:

> When I came to the Rebekah Home for Girls, I needed all the help I could get. . . . I was very rebellious and wouldn't take anything from them [her parents]. . . . At the Rebekah Home I felt loved and protected. I was taught the Word of God and I learned it. I cannot remember one time feeling unloved. There was so much love in the home and such a sweet spirit. . . . Only by the grace of God am I alive today. All it took to keep me alive was love—the love of God. I saw it in Brother Roloff and the people at the Rebekah Home. Brother Roloff stands for the truth, and he doesn't compromise.

Lester went to school in a one-room schoolhouse called "headquarters." "I had three favorite subjects," he likes to tell. "Three R's—running, 'restling, and recess!" His teacher predicted he would have a career on stage since he was the class comedian. Stage presence has always come naturally to him; there has never been a time in his life when he wasn't at ease pacing back and forth on a platform, microphone in hand, speaking to an audience and holding their attention.

Lester concedes that he was unusually successful in convincing his teachers not to punish him all the way through school. He was particularly in his element when he was telling funny stories. He still holds the attention of his audiences with his comic illustrations.

On Christmas Day, 1973, when my husband was handed a five-day jail sentence, fined $5,400, and cited for contempt of court, he reflected on those school days. "As an ignorant, freckle-faced country boy, I used to stand in a one-room schoolhouse, where one teacher taught all eight grades after she had ridden five miles to school on an old crow-hopping horse, and sing, 'Our father's God, to Thee, Author of Liberty, to Thee we sing: Long may our land be bright, with freedom's holy light; protect us by Thy might, Great God, our King!' I am not a flag burner, and I still believe in what Old Glory stands for, but I wonder how long it will be before we can say again, 'with liberty and justice for *all.*' "

14

Surrender!

He was timid, blond, blue-eyed, and frail at age seventeen. Recurring sick spells plagued him even then; they would give him trouble in the college years ahead.

One night he felt especially ill and went to bed early. He lay in bed, alone and afraid. He was unlearned in many Bible teachings and understood little of the leading and working of the Holy Spirit. As his mother started toward the old-fashioned telephone to call the doctor, he called out to her, "Mama, it's not that doctor I need tonight."

There, in the long hall of the old ranch house, Lester Roloff promised God that if He would let him live, the sun would come up the next morning on a young man who would surrender his life to being a preacher. When he got back in bed, great peace came over him; rest flooded his soul, and he slept better than he had in many months.

The next morning the sun was already up when he awoke. His father and brothers had gone to the fields to work. Lester had been left undisturbed because he had been so ill. He walked out to the well to get a drink of water, and as he looked out across the fields, he knew he must leave the old home place. He had one year of high school left, but after that he knew he must go somewhere to study the Bible. How could he preach without an education? How could he get an education without money? Where was he to go?

He faced many problems, but already he felt that God would somehow make a way. That day he told his parents about the call to preach. They said little even though they were astonished. He could hear them whispering when they thought he was asleep at night. . . . "Sally, he needs to go to college."

"Yes, Harry, he needs an education."

"Sally, it won't be easy."

"I know, I know, but God knows, too, Harry."

Lesters brothers frankly doubted the call. At times he was timid around strangers, and he refused to pray aloud in public. "How can Lester ever become a preacher?" they asked each other.

To complicate matters the Great Depression days hit the country about the time of Lester's high school graduation. There was no money to spare for anything, but Mama saved egg money and bought Lester his high school graduation ring. Years later, after graduation from Baylor, he had the ring made into a wedding band for his mother. "She more than deserved it," he told me with tears in his eyes and a quiver in his voice.

Those Depression days were days of great trial for almost everyone. Money, food, and clothing were scarce. Whenever the Roloffs acquired a suit, Melvin wore it until he outgrew it. Then Edell inherited it. Finally, Lester was allowed to own it.

On their way back home from Dawson one night Lester and Melvin heard the ominous POP, which meant a flat tire. The car was stopped, and the boys inspected the damaged tire. Then Melvin calmly removed his trousers and carefully placed them on the car seat until he had repaired the tire. Cleaning and mending trousers was an expensive task. Later, in thinking about this incident, Lester said, "I surely was glad Melvin was taking such good care of *our* trousers!"

Lester decided he wanted to get his education at Baylor University in Waco, Texas. To earn the entrance fees he worked on the farm for seven cents an hour and hauled hay for neighbors for seventy-five cents a day—four dollars and twenty-five cents a week. Then he went to West Texas, where he stayed with an aunt and uncle while he picked cotton for fifty cents a hundred pounds. A good day found him picking over four hundred pounds.

At the end of two months he was ready to go home. Before leaving, he went into town to buy his first new suit. He paid fifteen dollars for a coat and two pairs of trousers. Some of the joy of owning a new suit left him, however, when his aunt told him he had paid too much.

The trip home, hitching a ride with a man in a slow-moving old car, seemed to take forever. But, oh, how glorious it was to see the lights of home and greet his brothers and parents. Had he only been gone two months? It seemed an eternity! Recalling later the tremendous joy of this homecoming, he compared it to the joys of the Christian on reaching his eternal home and being welcomed by the heavenly Father and His Son.

Lester had earned enough money for entrance fees at Baylor, but he still had to consider room and board. He went to Waco with the idea of taking a cow and milking her in exchange for room and board. After approaching many rooming houses with this proposition, he found a family who agreed to let him stay if he could guarantee four gallons of milk a day. He found a place to keep the cow and returned home to discuss the plan with his father.

Papa viewed the idea with some misgivings at first, but eventually he consented to furnish the cow and the hay for feed. Papa and Lester loaded the cow and the feed into a trailer and headed for Baylor. "Marie" had the distinction of probably being the only cow in history to go to college!

Lester describes his freshman and sophomore years, saying, "At six o'clock each morning I met my cow down at the cow shed in the middle of the block where a big dormitory of girls now stands, and I would begin my day in prayer and milking."

When Lester's father needed to borrow money at the bank, he never had to sign a note. He knew nothing about collateral. When he needed money, he would go into the Dawson bank, approach Mr. Weaver or Mr. Newton, and state, "I would like to borrow about a thousand dollars until I get my crops laid by." The response would be, "Sure, Harry."

Before Lester left for Baylor, his father made an arrangement with the bankers for his son to sign checks on his own bank account should an emergency arise while Lester was away in school. The bankers looked at Lester and said, "Son, we hope you'll be as honest a man as your father is. Harry's word is as good as his bond."

Money was described in those times as being "as scarce as hen's teeth." Lester has always referred to himself as a freshman who was "socially timid, intellectually dumb, and financially busted." He soon became known, however, for what he called his "theme song." He went around campus singing and humming the song "Keep in Touch with Jesus." As Lester faced trials and temptations, he remembered, *"Keep in touch with Jesus; He will keep you sweet."*

As he looked at the other students on campus, many of whom had problems and were lonely, he remembered, *"You perhaps can bring them joy and peace complete. Keep in touch with Jesus; He will keep you sweet."*

It was his desire to be a blessing to others; he longed to convey love to the students and teachers; and he was reminded, *"Let the Holy Spirit overcome defeat. Keep in touch with Jesus; He will keep you sweet."* The words came to mind often, and each time they buoyed him. *"Would you have communion with your Lord each day? Have a blessed union with Him all the way? Praying without ceasing, learning at his feet? Keep in touch with Jesus; He will keep you sweet."*

This explains to my satisfaction the sweetness of my husband's spirit: Lester has always kept in touch with Jesus.

He was to need this close touch in the four years of college. Physically he was still not strong. Periodically he had sideache attacks, a forewarning of appendicitis. He realized that sooner or later he might have to yield to the uncomfortable and costly experience of an appendectomy. The more he thought of this, the more he decided he wanted it to be "later"!

His room and board at college were being taken care of by his faithful cow, but there was still the cost of books and other expenses that were encountered from time to time. One day he met a local doctor who had a number of delinquent bills on his books that no one had been able to collect. "Lester, you can have a certain percentage of the collections if you are able to make the people respond to your pleas for payments of their accounts." Even at this he was successful.

Classes at Baylor were interesting but difficult. Lester took them in stride, applied himself, and set about to make the most of his college years. As a freshman Lester was singularly honored when the class chose him as their speaker to represent them in chapel. He worked for days on the message. One of his professors helped him with the wording and smoothed out the rough edges. Lester memorized it and recited it to his cow. He stood in front of the mirror and practiced his delivery. He shut himself in the bathroom and preached to the bathroom fixtures. He practiced and practiced. When it came time to give the message, he was well-prepared, but the Holy Spirit took over as he poured his heart and entire spirit into what he was saying. Not surprisingly, it went well.

His back and side continued to give him pain. Finally, in desperation, in the fall of his sophomore year Lester consented to an appendectomy. For a time his health improved, then he began to have intermittent pains in his chest. X-rays were taken. The results were not encouraging. Dr. Ainsworth gave his diagnosis in no uncertain terms. "Lester, your heart is troubling you. You will *never* make it as a preacher. You are a sick boy. My advice to you is to go home, help on the farm, but don't overdo, and try to get well."

Lester was disturbed, but he was a determined young man. In his kind way and with characteristic humility he replied, "Dr. Ainsworth, the Lord knows more about me than you do because He made me. He wouldn't have called me to preach if He didn't intend to have me preach. I've got to stay on at the college." His faith was increasing daily. Even then God was preparing him for greater service than his finite mind could dream possible.

He began harder and harder to achieve better health, and he participated in many student activities. He preached at the old folks' home, in jails, on the street, and whenever he was asked. Soon he was asked to help pastor several small churches that could afford only the services of a half- or quarter-time preacher. They were small churches and the pay was little, but the practice for an aspiring preacher was great.

He thrust himself into every possible activity with all the

fervor his health could muster. Soon he began feeling stronger. God was honoring his faith and his efforts. He became an associate member of the Volunteer Band, a missionary organization on campus, and he was always faithful in attending the morning prayer group called "The Master's Minority." He was an active athlete, winning the marble-shooting championship three years in succession and the handball championship in singles and doubles competition in his junior and senior years. He also played forward on the winning ministerial basketball team in intramural athletics.

His popularity with classmates was recognized, and he never lacked for dates. The fact that he had no money to spare did not hinder his social activities—he attended church services, parties on campus, and group activities of his class. His joyous spirit won the respect of classmates. By now he had also become an interesting conversationalist. He was committed to serving Christ with all his heart, mind, and soul.

15

The Encounter

With his ever-increasing responsibilities as a weekend preacher Lester could leave behind his cow Marie when he went back to Baylor for his junior year.

That year he had three roommates who were to play important roles in his future—Joe Underwood, George Stewart, and Harold Fickett, Jr. The four ministerial students became the best of friends.

The summer between Lester's second and third years at Baylor was especially full. He was busy with work on the farm, at churches, and in revival meetings. Harold Fickett, however, decided Lester wasn't too busy to meet a friend of his. By coincidence, this friend's first name was Marie, but she wasn't four legged.

Harold had spoken to me many times about this paragon of a roommate he had at college. But the more Harold extolled Lester's good nature, his many abilities, and his other admirable traits, the more determined I became that I didn't want to meet him. No one could be that perfect! I really wasn't interested in meeting this Lester Roloff.

I must confess that one reason for my disinterest was that Lester was studying to be a preacher. I had never dated a preacher before although I'd known a good many of them in college. I considered them to be over-pious sissies who were afraid to do a day's work and who seemed to have the idea that the world owed them a living. No thanks, I wasn't going to have any part of a preacher!

Harold's father was pastor of our First Baptist Church in Galveston, Texas. During the entire summer of 1935, all I ever heard from Harold Fickett was "Lester Roloff." Harold and I were working in the same department in Sunday School and Training Union, and we ran into each other frequently in other church activities. I dreaded bumping into him. When Harold went back to Baylor to board with his roommate, I was glad to see him go!

Lester was also building up resistance to meeting me; Harold was annoyingly persistent. Finally Harold found the perfect solution. He discovered that both of us were planning to attend the State Training Union Convention held each year during the Thanksgiving holidays. That year the meeting was to be held at the First Baptist Church in Dallas. Harold dared Lester to write me a letter asking me to meet him there. Of course Lester was the type who couldn't say no to that kind of a dare.

The letter that arrived from Lester strangely intrigued me. I talked it over with my parents. Should I agree to meet Harold's roommate at the convention in Dallas? I responded to Lester saying that I'd be glad to meet him. Then he wrote a second time telling me what time to meet him at the entrance to the church. As far as I can remember, that is the first and only time I ever arrived at a meeting thirty minutes early! I did that so I could look him over. If I liked what I saw, I would carry out the plan; if not, I would fade into the crowd and stand him up!

He was of average height and neatly attired in a navy blue suit with vest, navy tie, and white shirt. He wore a hat and glasses. Since it was November and a rather brisk wind was blowing, he carried an overcoat over his arm. I wasn't sure this fine-looking, blond-haired young man was the fellow I was to meet, but I couldn't help hoping he was!

I had heard his name so many times that I had become tired of it. But now that I was about to meet him, I wasn't even sure I could pronounce it correctly. I decided to give it a try. Taking a deep breath, I opened the door of the church and approached him. "Excuse me, but are you waiting for someone?"

He looked at me, smiled, and answered, "Why, yes, I am. Are you Marie Brady?"

From that point on we attended all the sessions of the convention together.

Lester felt he needed to sit with his church people, and that's what we did. I thought to myself that if I didn't enjoy being with him, it would be easy to bow out gracefully. As the morning progressed, however, I found myself enjoying every minute of sitting next to him.

When noontime came, Lester had made arrangements for the church members to go one way, and he and I went another. This was going to be our time together to talk and get acquainted. We went to the Mayflower Hotel, and Lester ordered a beautiful Thanksgiving dinner for us. We slowly walked back to the afternoon session, but I must admit I heard very little of those messages.

On Saturday, the final day of the convention, we were both conscious that we had precious few moments left to spend together. Lester left with his church members before my train pulled out for Galveston. I must have touched my cheek a hundred times where he kissed me when we parted. Already I missed him, so I sat down and wrote him a letter.

When Lester arrived in Waco on Monday, he had a ten-page letter waiting for him. Thus began our correspondence, with letters going back and forth once a week, then twice a week, then three times weekly, and finally one every day.

Then came Christmas. Lester decided to accompany

Harold home to Galveston for the holidays. This time neither of us had to be coaxed to see each other. Of course Harold reminded us often that he had had a part in our meeting each other!

My husband is fond of telling that when we first met I told him I would never marry a preacher. He had replied that he didn't mind, for his plans didn't include a wife in the near future. But now those plans suddenly changed! During the holidays he asked me to marry him. I wasn't too surprised and quickly answered yes.

Lester was an old-fashioned young man. He went to my parents to receive their permission to marry me. That same Sunday Lester brought the evening message at our church and sang. It was the first time I had heard him preach or sing—Christmas, 1935.

In February at our church's annual Sweetheart Banquet, our engagement announcement was made. It came in the form of a telegram delivered during the course of the evening's events.

The wedding took place August 10, 1936, with Harold Fickett's father performing the ceremony. Lester and I were opposites in backgrounds and natures. I was an only child and a city girl. He used to say I did not know a cow from a horse or a chicken from a pig. But our mutual love for the Lord and for each other was deep and real.

He was still half-time pastor of two churches, Purdon and Navarro Mills. I often teased him that I was marrying him for his money. At that time he was receiving a total salary of fifty dollars a month.

During that summer preceding our wedding, Lester conducted revival meetings in many small Texas towns. I should have realized then, but I did not, that my husband was destined to be an evangelist. One little town after another was turned upside down by the preaching of this fiery Baylor student. These were wicked little towns where the gambling halls and liquor stores did a thriving business. In Purdon it was estimated that more than one hundred people were born again. The gambling hall closed and the bootlegger went out of business. Now it was necessary for the church to get a full-time pastor, and Navarro Mills had to find some other part-time pastor.

16

Heaven's Hitching Post

We were initiated into the pastorate during Lester's final year at Baylor. On weekends we traveled to Purdon. Our daughter, Elizabeth Ann, was born on June 20, 1937. That fact necessitated a raise for the pastor to one hundred dollars a month. At the time it seemed like a small fortune.

After graduation from Baylor we moved to Fort Worth where my husband could attend Southwestern Seminary. While there he was asked to be the pastor of the First Baptist Church of Trinidad, Texas. It was a hundred-mile trip from Fort Worth to Trinidad—a long, wearisome drive with a small child. In retrospect, however, we view those years as some of the happiest of our lives.

Performing funerals and weddings, going on visitation, carrying on personal soul-winning, pouring oil on troubled church waters—all of these things and more consumed my husband's time on those busy weekends. The message my husband preached then is essentially the same one he preaches now. He fought sin in all of its expressions and manifestations. He still does. He believed, and still does, in the sanctity of the church, the home, and the school. His loyalty to his country and his strong belief in the rights of the individual have never changed.

When my husband stood behind the pulpit, I knew with wifely pride that the people in the audience would hear a message from the Word of God. "Give me an open mind, a hungry heart, and a sincere soul," he would plead. "All that

I am, have been, or ever hope to be that's worthwhile and that God can bless is based and founded upon the truths found in this Book," and he would hold the Bible aloft. "Whatever blessing I may be to you stems from and is flavored with the aroma of the gospel that I preach in this sermon." And then he would launch into a message profound in its simplicity, yet powerful in its impact.

I'm not asking you to consider this message from the standpoint of its logic or its profoundness or its homiletical arrangement but from the standpoint of the many precious Scriptures that the Lord has been pointing out to me. In this day when Christianity has gone from shouts to doubts and from its shine to the shadows, and from its "I know" to "I wish," "I wonder," or "I hope so," we need security. I've asked God for wisdom, sincerity, and simplicity as I share with you what's on my heart.

Religion without righteousness is a racket. Instead of hobbling our religious horse, we need to tie him to the hitching post of eternal truth. Every joy and every hope I have revolves itself around and anchors itself to the hitching post of salvation by grace.

Ecclesiastes 3:14 says, "I know that, whatsoever God doeth, it shall be for ever: nothing can be put to it, nor any thing taken from it: and God doeth it, that men should fear before him."

Salvation is from the Lord. "For by grace are ye saved through faith; and that not of yourselves: it is the gift of God: Not of works, lest any man should boast. For we are his workmanship, created in Christ Jesus unto good works, which God hath before ordained that we should walk in them" (Eph. 2:8-10).

"Not by works of righteousness which we have done, but according to his mercy he saved us, by the washing of regeneration, and renewing of the Holy Ghost; Which he shed on us abundantly through Jesus Christ our Saviour; That being justified by his grace, we should be made heirs according to the hope of eternal life" (Titus 3:5-7).

His messages were always laced with Scripture that carried the hearer along from one logical point to another.

Salvation is wholly of the Lord. God thought it, Jesus bought it, the Spirit wrought it, the Bible taught it, old Satan fought it, but thank God, I've got it; and more than anything else, I want you to have it. If you are not sure of your salvation, may this message put the eternal clamps of truth on your soul and anchor you securely to heaven's hitching post, namely, salvation by grace.

Whether he took his hearers into the Old Testament or into the New Testament, Lester pointed them toward the cross.

The condition of man demands salvation by grace. Psalm 53:2,3 says, "God looked down from heaven upon the children of men, to see if there were any that did understand, that did seek God." The answer, my friend, is, "Every one of them is gone back: they are altogether become filthy; there is none that doeth good, no, not one."

"All we like sheep have gone astray; we have turned everyone to his own way; and the Lord hath laid on him the iniquity of us all" (Isa. 53:6).

Micah raised the question, ". . . shall I give . . . the fruit of my body for the sin of my soul?" He answered it and said, ". . . what doth the Lord require of thee, but to do justly, and to love mercy, and to walk humbly with thy God?" (Mic. 6:7,8).

Man is spiritually dead without Christ. Ephesians 2:1: "And you hath he quickened, who were dead in trespasses and sins."

As he moved the listeners along with these convicting verses, he brought them to the feet of Jesus.

Jesus dealt with Nicodemus and said to him, ". . . Ye must be born again" (John 3:7). We have an *everlasting God* and an *eternal Christ* with *everlasting mercy* who offers *everlasting life* through an *everlasting Gospel.*

He had begun by stating that people today are searching for security. When he began his wrap-up, I knew he would come back to that.

We have security councils, we have social security, and man is making desperate efforts for security along every other line. And yet he is content to be uncertain about his salvation and his eternal destiny.

The apostle Paul said, "For I am persuaded, that neither death, nor life, nor angels, nor principalities, nor powers, nor things present, nor things to come, Nor height, nor depth, nor any other creature, shall be able to separate us from the love of God, which is in Christ Jesus our Lord" (Rom. 8:38,39).

He also said in 2 Corinthians 5:17, "Therefore if any man be in Christ, he is a new creature: old things are passed away; behold, all things are become new." Paul never exercised doubt about his salvation. When they told him it was time for the chopping block, he said, "For I am now ready. . . . I have fought a good fight, I have finished *my* course, I have kept the faith: Henceforth there is laid up for me a crown of righteousness, which the Lord, the righteous judge, shall give me at that day: and not to me only, but unto all them also that love His appearing" (2 Tim. 4:6-8).

Wouldn't you agree with me that nobody ever gets saved by circumcision or baptism or church membership or good works? The writer of Hebrews tells us, "So Christ was once offered to bear the sins of many . . ." (Heb. 9:28).

The gifts and calling of God are for you. Salvation is a gift. There's a difference in the cost of salvation and the cost of discipleship. It cost God all He had to send it, Jesus all He had to bring it, the sinner nothing to accept it, but the Christian all to live it. I do not work in order to be saved but because I am saved. I do not support my wife and child in order to be her husband and the baby's daddy but because I am.

17

Testing Times

The world was at war. The war to end all wars—World War I—had left many problems unsolved. The rise of dictatorships and the desire of countries like Germany, Italy, and Japan for more territory brought on World War II. It opened the Atomic Age and saw more than fifty countries take part in the fighting. The whole world felt the effects of this war. It killed more persons, cost more money, damaged more property, affected more people, and caused more far-reaching changes than any other war in history.

The war brought changes our way too. We moved to Houston, Texas, where my husband became pastor of Magnolia Park Baptist Church. The church was located in the east end of the city, an area of great spiritual need. Many of the people were defense workers in the Houston shipyards or at the Hughes Tool Company. Houston, too, was caught in turmoil. Never shall we forget the bombing of Pearl Harbor by the Japanese on Sunday, December 7, 1941.

More and more women left their homes to work in wartime industries. New responsibilities arose concerning broken homes. Young men from the church were shipped overseas. Then began the sad task of dealing with homes where gold stars were hanging in the windows—heart-breaking symbols that a loved one had given his life in the service of his country. Special prayer services were held for the boys overseas. The church doors were always open so people might go in and pray at any time for our men in uniform. The list of these men, which hung in the church for all to see, kept growing. It was a time of deep concern.

Africa, Europe, Asia, and the Pacific — we followed the news in the papers and via radio. Churches united in prayer for world-wide peace. My husband participated with representatives from all faiths in one such mass meeting at Houston's Memorial Coliseum.

The church grew by leaps and bounds. It was a time of great revival with hundreds being born again. We were happy in the work at Magnolia Park. Three glorious years had endeared the people to us. And then the pulpit committee from the Park Avenue Baptist Church in Corpus Christi, Texas, called and invited my husband to consider becoming their pastor.

"My work isn't finished in Houston," my husband said to me, and then he added, "but, Marie, we have to be open to the bidding of the Holy Spirit."

The visit to Corpus Christi was challenging. Many Navy men and their families were stationed there at the largest naval air station in the world. "It's a field ripe for harvest," Lester declared. But he was torn. "We must wait on the Lord," he reminded me. "We will pray and listen for the Lord's leading. I am ready to go, but I am ready to stay."

The answer came—as it always does when we seek God's leading. But I was heartbroken. The day we moved from Houston, there was a torrential rainfall. My husband said later that it was raining as much inside the car as it was outside. The rain on the inside, however, subsided after a time. I was able to tell my husband, "Lester, '. . . I have learned, in whatsoever state I am, therewith to be content'" (Phil. 4:11).

The first six months in the new pastorate brought both joy

and sorrow, happiness and pain. It was to be in the city of Corpus Christi (the name means "Body of Christ") that we would meet our largest challenges. Here our roots were to go down deep, and experiences were to come that would plumb the depths of human emotion.

We had seen and been told by those in the ministry that in almost every church there are some who are fractious and contentious. My husband had been warned in seminary that at times there will be "a noise of war in the camp." We knew that the "ministerial honeymoon" does not last forever in a new church situation. We had heard about individuals who have the reputation of "running off" pastors, causing them to resign. But even with all these warnings, we were not ready for the rumblings of an earthquake in the ranks of some of our deacons. But the church did not realize that my husband was a fighter and not a quitter. "Marie," he said to me, "I wasn't called to preach by the people; God didn't send us here so that by the whim of a few discontents the church should suffer and the work fail to move forward."

And the church grew. The auditorium was filled to overflowing every Sunday. Even the pastor's study had to be used to accommodate the overflow crowd.

Loudspeakers were installed in the basement, and regular members of the church were encouraged to listen to the services down there so that guests and new members could fill the sanctuary auditorium. Still more room was needed.

When Lester first came to Park Avenue Church, none of the Baptist churches in Corpus Christi had a visitation program. He asked the women to visit on Thursday mornings and the men on Thursday nights. He instituted an all-night prayer meeting every Saturday night to make earnest petitions to God for the services the next day. He had begun the same plan of visitation and prayer in Houston and had seen the results there. Now we were seeing those same answers to visitation and prayer in Corpus Christi. But even more important was the presence of the Holy Spirit. At every service the convicting power was present, souls were saved, fellowship was restored, and believers were built up in the faith.

The Sunday School experienced the same amazing growth. The surge in enrollment and attendance was overwhelming. The dissenting deacons declared an armistice. Plans were drawn for a new educational building; the groundbreaking service was held, and the building's foundation was lined off so construction could begin.

Then came Sunday, October 15, 1944. Every spare foot of space was crowded as usual. My husband's text for that morning service was taken from 1 Kings 18:38, "Then the fire of the Lord fell. . . ." His sermon subject was "Let the Fire Fall."

At the close of the morning service Lester thought he smelled smoke in the building. But we dismissed it—his imagination was no doubt playing tricks on him after that message. He and some of the men searched the building but nothing of a suspicious nature was found. We went home for lunch.

We had just finished our meal when the phone rang: "The church is on fire!" Lester rushed to the church. It seemed the entire population of the city was already there. Later it was determined that the fire had been smoldering before it burst into flames. My husband's earlier suspicions of smoke had not been just a figment of his imagination.

Nothing could be done to save the building. Gone in a short time were a new organ, a grand piano, new carpets, and other major improvements that had been made. They were all turned to ashes. Efforts were made to save the other buildings, and two were spared. Later they became the church office and the Park Avenue Day School.

That Sunday evening the congregation met beside the still-smoldering ashes. Everyone was in a state of shock. But people met Christ that night, including one small boy, Leslie Warren, who is now a missionary.

Then began a time of testing as the church began to meet in a local junior high school. A new church building had to be built. But where? The former site seemed undesirable due to a lack of parking facilities and room for growth. A search was begun. But once again internal dissension rocked the church body. A group of church members wrote a letter and circulated it among other members. Exaggerated charges were brought against my husband. One dear saint called and said, "Pastor, wrap yourself in Psalm 91."

He that dwelleth in the secret place of the most High shall abide under the shadow of the Almighty.

I will say of the Lord, He is my refuge and my fortress: my God, in him will I trust.

Surely he shall deliver thee from the snare of the fowler, and from the noisome pestilence.

He shall cover thee with his feathers, and under his wings shalt thou trust: his truth shall be thy shield and buckler.

Thou shalt not be afraid for the terror by night; nor for the arrow that flieth by day;

Nor for the pestilence that walketh in darkness; nor for the destruction that wasteth at noonday.

A thousand shall fall at thy side, and ten thousand at thy right hand; but it shall not come nigh thee.

Only with thine eyes shalt thou behold and see the reward of the wicked.

Because thou hast made the Lord, which is my refuge, even the most High, thy habitation;

There shall no evil befall thee, neither shall any plague come nigh thy dwelling.

For he shall give his angels charge over thee, to keep thee in all thy ways.

They shall bear thee up in their hands, lest thou dash thy foot against a stone.

Thou shalt tread upon the lion and adder: the young lion and the dragon shalt thou trample under feet.

Because he hath set his love upon me, therefore will I deliver him: I will set him on high, because he hath known my name.

He shall call upon me, and I will answer him: I will be with him in trouble; I will deliver him, and honor him.

With long life will I satisfy him, and shew him my salvation.

What comfort there was in that Psalm for both of us, and how we needed it! Many times since then we have fled to that "secret place of the most High." What a refuge there is for the Christian "under the shadow of the Almighty."

A meeting was called, and it was moderated by a Houston friend. The outcome of the meeting of church members was a favorable majority for my husband. The dissenting members left the church. Once again we began to function as a united body of believers.

Lester was being called upon more and more to hold revival meetings and evangelistic services in Corpus Christi churches and elsewhere. He organized the Baptist Ministerial Alliance in Corpus Christi and served as its first president. Those days were busy and fulfilling for all of us.

That December the Lord blessed our home with another

baby girl—this one by adoption. Elizabeth Ann, our first-born, was now seven years old. Pamela Kay found a place in our hearts from the beginning.

I watched as my husband's faith soared. Daily he was being called upon to exercise that faith in unexpected ways. "Faith never loiters nor lounges in the shadows," he preached. "Faith never follows the fickle crowd on the fringes nor to where comforts and pleasure lead. Faith neither wears a crown nor displays any medals. Faith is a fighter. The rewards and the medals come after the battle is done and the victory is won."

18

Birth of a Broadcast

On May 8, 1944, with fear and trembling and yet with great determination, my husband walked into a little 250-watt radio station to begin a daily fifteen-minute broadcast. Even before moving to Corpus Christi Lester had felt God's call to begin such a broadcast. One of the conditions he made when we moved to Park Avenue Baptist was that such a radio ministry be started. The church was not ready to launch into such a program by faith; but the deacons did agree to pledge half the payment, and we were to be responsible for the other half.

This was a tremendous step of faith. We had no income other than the pastoral salary; but Lester possessed the confidence to believe that if God were in this, He would provide the necessary financial resources. "Doesn't the Scripture say, 'Now the just shall live by faith'?" he asked me. Thus was born the Family Altar Program, a daily time of spiritual refreshment, Bible study, and prayer.

After the program had been on the air four years, we were told we were going to be put off the station because Lester insisted on preaching against definite sins. Actually he was preaching against the evils of alcohol while at the same time the radio station was accepting advertising from the liquor industry.

About this time a certain lawyer in the city challenged Lester to a debate on the subject. The debate was held in Buccaneer Stadium. From the outset, however, the lawyer was on the losing side because he showed up too drunk to defend his viewpoint.

But the radio station issued an ultimatum—either keep quiet about the evils of drinking intoxicating beverages, or take the radio program to another station. Lester chose the latter.

The day after we went off that station, we went on a 50,000-watt station, KWBU. (The last letters stand for Baylor University.) Lester often refers to that day as "the day we cut our spiritual teeth to walk by faith."

The radio ministry continued to be a faith venture, and he came to depend more and more on Paul's statement in Hebrews 10:38 about the just living by faith. There was no turning back. The message went out over the air waves to first one station and then another, first in the coastal states, and then in the north, south, east, and west. The program grew to include Hawaii and foreign countries.

The radio bills mounted with the increased station coverage. Lester talks about those early years of pioneering the radio ministry as years of "trials, tears, temptations, and testings." My husband enjoys music, and when things were particularly worrisome, I'd hear him singing, "The answer you have prayed for is on its way and paid for, so hold on a little longer, hold on!" And he would hold on.

Or I'd hear him singing, "From victory unto victory, His army shall He lead, Till every foe is vanquished, and Christ is Lord indeed."[2]

In times of discouragement he would repeat the motto, "Praise God anyhow." Circumstances couldn't defeat him. "God's watch tells eternity; my watch tells time," he'd say. "Man is looking for a better plan; God is looking for a

---

[2]George Duffield, "Stand Up For Jesus."

better man." And then I'd hear him pray: "Lord, help me to be that man. Help me to remember that my times are in Thy hands."

One favorite Scripture that encouraged him often is Isaiah 40:31: "But they that wait upon the Lord shall renew their strength; they shall mount up with wings as eagles; they shall run, and not be weary; and they shall walk, and not faint."

The fact that the Bible says our strength shall be renewed implies there will be times when it is weakened, when we do not feel like running, when we are weary and faint. What an encouragement that was to Lester; what an encouragement it can be to all of us.

"God is able to do exceeding abundantly above all that we ask or think," he would remind radio listeners. He was preaching to himself as much as to them. "I've seen God vindicate His Word in our ministry," he'd say, his voice quivering with emotion. "I've seen God stand by the one who preaches it and honor the faith of those who believe it."

The radio ministry gained a following of all ages. To the children he became "Uncle Rollie" as he related much-loved Bible stories. To the elderly he was reminiscent of the times under the old brush arbors where they had been saved or had come to rededicate their lives. Many of the older songs had been relegated to the past; the Family Altar Program helped to revive them. Shut-ins received a special blessing from hearing the Word read as did those whose eyesight was failing and who could no longer read the Bible for themselves. Many times Lester chose to read entire chapters, and then he would bring a short simple message urging the hearers to "keep on keeping on" and to "stay by the stuff." And the listening audience grew and grew.

The church services felt the impact of the radio audience. People would drive for miles to see and hear their radio pastor. The reaction was always the same: "Brother Roloff, you do not look at all as I had pictured you." My husband is a slightly-built man, standing five feet ten. But his voice is resonant and deep, and his delivery is dynamic and forceful.

At the outset of the radio ministry Lester let it be known that he would stand unwaveringly for the truth of the Word of God. "The message will always be the same—a message of Calvary, the virgin birth, the sinless life, the wonderful atonement, the bodily resurrection, and the glorious return of our Savior. I'll keep back nothing, but declare the whole counsel of God."

19

Conviction or Compromise

In November, 1945, there occurred in Lester's life a meeting of far-reaching significance. Baylor University had decided to present President Harry S. Truman with an honorary degree. Truman was noted, among other things, for his rough language. My husband was chairman of the Baylor Civil Rights Platform Committee, and he felt it was inappropriate for a Baptist college to honor a man who failed to uphold Bible standards and convictions in his daily life. Under strong conviction about this matter Lester went before the Baptist General Convention of Texas to propose a motion that would in effect place a restricting hand on Baylor University and advise the school to choose someone else to receive that honorary degree. The convention was divided in its vote, but the final result was that Baylor did award the degree to President Truman as planned.

As I think back to that difficult time, I would have to say that this was probably the beginning of the end as far as Lester's loyalty to the denomination was concerned. He had no use for compromise. He felt that a man must remain true to his convictions no matter what the cost. His stand brought much publicity—some good, some bad. He received an inquiry from the A. N. Marquis Company of Chicago, Illinois. The following April my husband appeared in *Who's Who in America.*

About this same time he began to receive anonymous phone calls and unsigned hate mail. Still, the church in

Corpus Christi continued to grow. Some of the Baptist brethren were not too friendly; some did not understand the issues at stake, nor Lester's deep convictions. Requests to hold revival meetings came less frequently. Lester was no longer being called upon for committee work in the Baptist General Convention of Texas, but college friends he had known well soared ahead in their positions of responsibility within the Convention. My husband was paying a price for his convictions.

"Marie," he confided, 'The grass withereth, the flower fadeth: but the word of our God shall stand for ever' (Isa. 40:8). I must stand on what I believe the Word is saying to me."

To the faithful radio listeners he could say:

I've been visiting Brother David in 2 Samuel 22, and I've heard him recite his Psalm of thanksgiving. David's soul was filled with praise for what the Lord had done. Along with him I, too, can say, "The Lord is my rock and my fortress, and my deliverer; The God of my rock; in Him will I trust: He is my shield, and the horn of my salvation, my high tower, and my refuge, my saviour; thou savest me from violence." (2 Sam. 22:2,3). God is my strength, my power, my lamp, my buckler.

What a glorious testimony we have in the Word coming from the lips of a man who had gone through deep waters. He had seen members of his own family turn against him; he had been forced to leave the palace and live in exile. But in the end, the Lord gave the victory.

No wonder David said, "In my distress I called upon the Lord, and cried to my God: and He did hear my voice out of his temple . . . . He drew me out of many waters; He delivered me from my strong enemy, and from them that hated me; for they were too strong for me. . . . He brought me forth also into a large place: He delivered me, because He delighted in me" (2 Sam. 22:7,17,18,20).

The secret of David's deliverance is in these verses, "For I have kept the ways of the Lord, and have not wickedly departed from my God. For all His judgments were before me: and as for His statutes, I did not depart from them. . . . For thou art my lamp, O Lord: and the Lord will lighten my darkness. For by thee I have run through a troop: by my God have I leaped over a wall. As for God, His way is perfect; the Word of the Lord is tried: He is a buckler to all them that trust in Him" (2 Sam. 22:22,23,29-31).

My husband was being pressured to let up in his stand. He was being urged to back up and even give up. Many times I saw his cheeks wet with tears as he saw lifetime friends slip away. One friend wrote and asked for money back that he had invested in the radio ministry. "I've made a bad investment," he wrote. My husband sent the money back. But two years later that same man sent it to the ministry again, saying he had been wrong and wanted to support the kind of gospel my husband was faithfully preaching.

"I cannot beat a retreat," my husband would say, "nor compromise the message. Let's just thank God and take courage."

For six years he held firm in his stand. Then, in 1954, he was removed from the station KWBU because he was considered too controversial. Lester said at the time, "This is the most crushing disappointment in all of my twenty-one years of ministry. In some ways it seems that we have reached the end of our gospel trail."

My husband is human, and he was deeply hurt. But the Lord knew this ultimatum was coming; the station was owned and operated by the Baptist General Convention of Texas. In the Lord's providence precious friends had given and loaned to us $50,000 to go on three stations in Houston, San Antonio, and Fort Worth. For almost eleven years Lester had been living with a microphone around his neck, getting out the messages via radio, and now God in His goodness was going to see to it that the program was kept on the air uninterrupted. The Fort Worth program did not materialize at that time, but there were numerous other areas that began to open up. "Instead of quitting or curtailing the broadcast work," Lester announced, "we will, with God's leadership, press on."

A change in station policy conveniently removed him from another station. Obviously the devil and his hosts didn't want the Family Altar Program on the air. Letters were coming to him relating miraculous conversion experiences. One such report came from Houston where a woman, convicted of murder, heard the program from her jail cell and asked Christ to save her. With results like that we knew Satan's attacks would continue.

Not many months later the KWBU station was put up for sale. The owners had lost $70,000 in one year and were anxious to sell. The price, however, was $300,000. "We don't have it," Lester told me. I already knew that. But in his next breath he added, "But with the help of God and His people we'll get it." I knew that too.

Such was the spirit of my husband regardless of the circumstances. I shall never forget when the lawyer Harry Dobbs and I had to go to the bank and sign papers to negotiate the loan for the purchase of the station. Lester was out of town and $25,000 was needed as earnest money.

Another $100,000 was needed ninety days later. On the last day Lester had all of it but $7,250. In the last hour all he needed was $250! Forty-five minutes before the deadline it was *all* there! Others became stockholders and actually became the station's owners, but my husband was the vehicle God chose to use to get that station into the right hands. Today the station is still in operation with the call letters KCTA—Know Christ the Answer. In most areas of the country, the Family Altar Program is aired twice daily and once on Sunday afternoons.

Support for the radio ministry came in strange and unexpected ways. One listener dedicated twenty acres of his land to the work. In one season more than $20,000 worth of produce was sold from that dedicated soil. When my husband shared this on the broadcast, he said, "Some of you are hearing the gospel because one consecrated farmer dedicated some acres to the preaching of the gospel."

That sparked a lot of interest among listeners who responded with creative projects to help get the Word out. One lady had what she called "consecrated hens" and gave her egg money. Another farmer had a cow from which came one calf each year; that cow sent out many broadcasts. A mother wrote, "You tell it; we'll pay it," and she and her daughter have long been among the most loyal supporters of the program.

"In this work," my husband would tell listeners, "I've been reminded time after time that we are not blessed for our successes, but for our faithfulness.

20

Mountains, Dreams, and Prayer

Jesus was the world's biggest misfit. He failed to fit into the religious systems of His day, into the political systems of His day, into the social systems of His day. Financially He was broke, and at the close of what seemed to be an untimely ministry, He didn't have even a lawyer to represent Him in Pilate's judgment hall. Scarcely a handful stood on Golgotha with bleeding hearts while He shed His atoning blood for a lost world. When He said, "It is finished," the world thought He was finished. But, praise God, there was another day that proved that Truth crushed to earth will rise again. On the resurrection morning the strong soldiers fell back like dead men when Jesus was raised "through the blood of the everlasting covenant" (Heb. 13:20).

This was the kind of preaching that saw the radio ministry move forward from that time on. "The just shall live by faith" was becoming a familiar refrain with Brother Roloff, and more than one letter writer commented about it.

This is the key to heaven's strongbox. Every prayer draft has been honored at the bank of faith, signed in the name of Jesus, because the Word is true. We've crossed Red Seas, enjoyed manna from heaven, drunk water from the Rock, followed the pillar of cloud by day and slept under the pillar of fire by night, eaten quail from the east, crossed old Jordan, shouted down Jericho, and I find myself saying even today, with Caleb of old, "Lord, give us this mountain."

We needed a new church building and some of us had been dreaming about starting a Christian day school. These were our "mountains" in late 1946. Prompted by his usual vision, Lester and the church board moved ahead and purchased property. Soon construction began. The first Sunday in the new large auditorium it seemed as though the entire congregation could have been seated in the choir loft with room to spare! Where were the people?

Now came another testing time. This was followed by an interval of intense prayer and visitation. Lester encouraged his "flock" by reminding them of God's faithfulness if they would do their part and witness and "go out into the high-ways and byways" following God's command. Before long it was evident that God had *not* written "Ichabod" over the door of the new church. The Lord's name was being magnified, and souls were being saved. More and more people decided to make Second Baptist their church home.

But the dream for a Christian day school persisted. Mrs. Walter Davis and I became the first teachers in the two-room school that began in the fall of 1946 in a little building that had been left after the church building had burned. The two classes of first grade were full from the beginning. Obviously the need for such a school existed, and the next year there was a demand for a second and third grade. Mrs. Gene Price (then Miss Frances Goodman) joined us in teaching and then worked as Lester's secretary in the afternoon. We were bulging at the seams, and we prevailed upon my husband to remedy the situation.

At about that time Lester was in the Rio Grande Valley preaching at a meeting. A friend in Raymondville asked him to pray with him for a much-needed rain for his cotton crop. Together the two men knelt in the field. That season the Lord superabundantly blessed that farmer. In gratitude he gave $10,000 and loaned another $10,000, and thus our Park Avenue Christian Day School was firmly established.

The school grew beyond even our wildest dreams, and it was my privilege to teach the first grade for seventeen years, and for several years I taught other grades.

Lester is fond of poetry and uses it often on the Family Altar broadcasts. I recall a poem that meant much to us in that time of our lives.

> I've dreamed many dreams that never came true,
> I've seen them vanish at dawn,
> But I've realized enough of my dreams, thank God
> To make me want to dream on.
>
> I've prayed many prayers when no answer came
> Tho' I've waited patient and long,
> But answers have come to enough of my prayers
> To make me keep praying on.[3]

We kept on dreaming and praying.

---

[3] Author unknown.

21

The Sawdust Trail

In the fall of 1950 Evangelist B. B. Crimm and his tent campaign came to Corpus Christi. Sawdust covered the floor, and we sat on rustic benches. During that campaign the evangelist was killed in an accident, and my husband was called to finish the meetings. While Lester was preaching those days, the Holy Spirit began to move in my husband's heart in a powerful way. He recognized what was happening. "Marie, I must yield to the leading of the Holy Spirit." But the conflict in his inner man waged—he loved his work at Second Baptist Church. The struggle continued for several months. I saw his body become weary from indecision. I counseled him to follow the leading of the Holy Spirit.

Finally, in April of 1951 he reached a decision. He preached his final message to the church and sang the song which was to be his theme song on the swawdust trail through the next four years as an evangelist and radio minister—"I'll Go Where You Want Me to Go, Dear Lord." It brought tears to the eyes of the church family that day, but there came a victory for Lester. He answered his "call into Macedonia."

Isaiah 54:2 became the promise upon which he built his evangelistic ministry. "Enlarge the place of thy tent, and let them stretch forth the curtains of thine habitations: spare not, lengthen thy cords, and strengthen thy stakes." As Lester told the congregation of his inward strivings, there was a stillness throughout the auditorium. At the invitation time the power of the Lord was felt, and people came to kneel at the altar.

The seven years at Second Baptist were a fruitful time—a time of seasoning, growing in wisdom, strengthening of convictions, and developing of a more fervent desire to see lost souls saved. The heartaches and disappointments had been the refiner's fire that burned off the dross and left the gold.

Evangelist Crimm's tent was bought, and Lester prepared to go on the road. Later, when Mr. and Mrs. E. A. Goodman began working with him, a larger tent without poles was built, and vans were purchased to haul the "canvas cathedral," chairs, platform, and equipment. Mr. W. D. York of Houston supplied a tractor and driver to pull the vans from meeting to meeting, in Texas, Georgia, Tennessee, Florida—wherever they were called. The work advanced by leaps and bounds, and Lester received more invitations than he could possibly accept.

As the tent meetings continued, the radio ministry also grew. Brother Goodman handled the tent, the recordings of the services, the duplication of tapes, and the mailings to the ever-growing list of stations across the country. Mrs. Goodman kept the radio logbook, and Frances Goodman Price managed the myriad of details connected with the Roloff Evangelistic Enterprises. My responsibility was to "stay by the stuff," teach at the Park Avenue Christian Day School, and maintain our home in Corpus Christi.

Every time Lester came home, he confided that he felt like an anchorless ship at sea with its motors dead. We were at another crossroads. Since he had been branded by the denominational leaders as "controversial," he felt at loose ends. "I have to plead guilty to being controversial," he said. "The truth is controversial. After all, Paul was branded a pestilent fellow, a mover of sedition, and a ringleader of the Nazarene sect. John Wesley was branded and excluded on charges of being undignified, unorthodox, and sensational. Elijah was called the troublemaker in Israel. Micaiah was hated by the king on the grounds that he would not say anything good about him. Amos, the country boy, was condemned for his porcupine preaching by Amaziah, evidently the president of the ministerial alliance in his city."

Lester needed a church home, a base from which to operate where there was a church family praying and supporting him with their love and concern. "Faith works today," he said to six friends who shared his feelings. "Faith never takes counsel with fear and never is a victim of circumstances." With that kind of faith $2,500 earnest money was put down on ten and four-tenths acres of land on South Alameda Street in Corpus Christi. God vindicated the decision on October 24, 1954 and the Alameda Baptist Church was organized. At three in the afternoon 126 people came for church membership, and within six months there were 374 members.

"These people have the sweetest spirit and the greatest vision for missions and service of any church we've ever served," he told his radio audience. "We have fewer wires strung, but God has given us of His Spirit." (We were meeting under the big gospel tent.) "We just want to win the lost for Christ," he emphasized.

The biggest step of faith occurred when the church took over the Good Samaritan Rescue Mission in Corpus Christi, assuming fifteen hundred dollars' worth of back debts. It was obvious that Lester's heart was overflowing as he ministered to these lost "sheep," feeding them and furnishing them a place to sleep.

The revival services continued with four major tent campaigns in various parts of the country each year—plus other gospel rallies, Bible conferences, and revivals. "It is our policy, under God's leadership, to go anywhere He leads; and while there, to seek to be a blessing to the local church, to win the lost, and to undergird the pastor's hands in his ministry."

The first issue of the publication to be entitled *Faith Enterprise* came out in May, 1955. "Romans 1:17 and Galatians 3:11 tells us that the just shall live by faith," Lester wrote. "The Bible doesn't say they could live or ought to live, but they shall live by faith. There are only two ways to live—one is by faith, the other by sight. Sight is the only way the natural man can live; but the just man shall live by faith, therefore giving evidence of his trust and confidence in God and thereby giving God an opportunity to unleash His power and make bare His mighty arm."

The *Faith Enterprise* became the way we could keep our radio listeners informed concerning the radio and revival schedules, the work of the church in Corpus Christi, the rescue mission, the day school, and any other reports and needs that arose. "When faith falters, we fail," he wrote. "Faith puts us into the realm of the righteous. Faith does the unusual, but faith is also practical. Jesus would still say if He came back to earth today, 'Be it done unto you according to your faith.' A man can live no better than by his faith in God."

22

Swan Song

On March 13, 1956, Lester stood in Waco Hall, Waco Texas, and spoke to more than two thousand people:

Twenty-three years ago, I entered this hall for the first time as a freshman in Baylor University. . . . For over two years my cow Marie and I put four gallons of milk on the boarding house table for my board and room while attending Baylor.

Those were wonderful days, and I am thankful for every revelation of truth that the Lord gave and for every contribution that the teachers made during those four years. . . .

In spite of the fact that no church in Waco would sponsor this meeting, there are over two thousand people present tonight [the auditorium seated twenty-five hundred]. My heart is encouraged and my soul is strengthened by your response to the truth. I'm grateful to the program committee that after all of the water that has run under the bridge and, of course, much that's run over the bridge, that you'd charge me with the responsibility of preaching this message in this hall tonight.

Here is the condition as I see it. Ecclesiasticism and denominational hierarchy have regimented and enslaved the people with the ultimatum you either bow or burn, and since most folks' faith is not fireproof, they acquiesce to the program. With love, and yet boldness, I have to say

that the average preacher is afraid of his own shadow. . .
The average preacher is afraid that he will not have any
place to preach. When John Wesley had no place to
preach, he stood on his father's tombstone in a cemetery
and in the face of being called sensational, undignified,
and irregular, preached a gospel that saved souls from sin.
He also rode saddle ponies to death with saddlebags filled
with Bibles and tracts. And now people have memorialized him by naming many churches after him.

Truth is never memorialized in the generation in which
it lives. Truth must serve a stretch on the scaffold before
it enters the throne room. Paul was called a pestilent
fellow. . . . And now the preacher stands on Sunday
morning with great dignity and reads with a pious voice,
"Saint Paul said . . ." And yet, if that old war horse were
to come back to this old crooked world, so saturated with
modernism, his ministry would have to be done outside
the average church. . . .

Old hot-tongued, leather-lunged, sun-scorched, desert-
bred John the Baptist didn't worry about a place to
preach. With a "preamp" in his left lung, the volume
control in his right lung, and an all-weather speaker in his
head he came bounding from the wilderness as Jesus'
bulldozer, leveling the hills of Judaism and jerking up the
stumps of formalism, saying, "Behold the Lamb of God,
which taketh away the sin of the world."

Dear old Brother Amos did not sit on a sycamore limb
waiting for a pulpit committee or a district missionary to
recommend him to some nice pastorate; but with his
preaching Bible in his hand, he headed for the city and
began to make trouble, He charged that they'd given the
Nazarites wine to drink, and he commanded the prophets
not to prophesy, saying that two cannot walk together

except they be agreed. He announced to them that God had cut off the rain and demanded that they prepare to meet God. Oh, what a parallel was his ministry to the need of this hour! He lifted his voice and cried, "Seek the Lord, and ye shall live . . ." (Amos 5:6).

The inevitable did happen when hatred arose and Amos announced that "They hate him that rebuketh in the gate, and they abhor him that speaketh uprightly" (Amos 5:10). Isaiah said the same thing, ". . . truth is fallen in the street, and equity cannot enter" (Isa. 59:14). Solomon said, "Wisdom crieth without . . ." (Prov. 1:20). Paul said, "Am I therefore become your enemy, because I tell you the truth?" (Gal. 4:16). Jesus, in Revelation 3:20, said, "I stand at the door, and knock."

Amos preached a negative gospel when he said, "Hate the evil and love the good . . ." (Amos 5:15). This old preacher with a brow of brass and nose of steel said, "I hate, I despise your feast days, and I will not smell in your solemn assemblies. . . . Woe to them that are at ease in Zion . . ." (Amos 5:21; 6:1). And he pulled the plumbline on that wicked city. Sure, he stirred up trouble.

Now, as I preach this message, don't waste any time trying to think up new anathemas to heap upon me. Some people look at me strangely and raise the question among their friends, "Well, what kind of Baptist is he?"

Well, I'll confess to you, dear friend, that I'm Jehovah's witness, a member of two churches of Christ—*the* church of Christ and *a* church of Christ. I'm a fundamentalist, a catholic priest, a member of the assembly of the first-born, a latter-day saint, a member of the Nazarene's church, and a Bible methodist. I believe in holiness apart from which no man can see the Lord, and I'm a seven-day adventist—I'm looking for him every day. And as far as a lot of Baptists are concerned, I guess I'm just a knothole Baptist; I'm on the outside but still seeing and saying what the Lord wants me to say which, when summed up, makes me a premillennial Southern Baptist, especially since I live in Corpus Christi with love for all and malice toward none.

I received an anonymous note in the mail saying that I reminded the writer of the appendix of a flea. After thinking it over I said, "Well, praise God, I'd rather be a live flea than a dead elephant." Besides, with the right kind of a bite, I believe one flea could wake up a pretty big dog. I read just this morning 1 Samuel 26:20 where King David called himself a flea. Just pray for me that I'll hop when and where God tells me to hop. Sometimes this denominational flea powder gets pretty strong!

In 1933 when we came to Baylor, we certainly were as green as grass, and the first thing we heard about the coming of the Lord from the Bible professor was, "I'm a 'Pro,' which means I'm for His coming." But when I came through Baylor and through the seminary in Fort Worth, I was taught actually the postmillennial theory, which means that this world will be converted, and by our preaching and missionary efforts we will usher in the golden age after which Jesus will come back to this old earth.

So I mounted the old gray horse of postmillennial preaching, and the longer I rode her, the weaker she got. She'd stumble every time I'd ride her very far into the Word of God, but when she would, I'd feed her a little more "professor hay" or a few more shucks of better-world building. When she'd try to balk, I'd just kick her with my spurs of denominational loyalty and exercise more faith in what I'd been taught—I'd preach a little louder. When I'd ride down Bible roads into Ezekiel, Daniel, or Matthew 13 and 14 or 24 and 25, the old gray mare would just shy away or completely stop. When I approached 1 and 2 Thessalonians and 1 and 2 Timothy, which have to do with the last days and the rapture, this old horse just ran away. As I saw sin on the increase and civilization shattered by vice and crime and violence, I determined in my soul that I'd get a running start against the wishes and advice of most of the preachers and professors and ride off into the book of Revelation with all the speed that I could get up. And when I finally got into chapter 19, verse 11, this old horse stumbled and fell; and I realized for the first time that I'd been riding the wrong horse anyhow. I looked up and saw the beautiful white horse and Jesus, the wonderful Word, in the saddle. So I left bridle, saddle, horse, and all.

It's been a real joy to ride the beautiful white horse of Revelation and speak boldly about the wonderful rapture and revelation of Jesus Christ. . . .

Now you may ask me why I became a premillennial preacher. I give you two reasons. In the first place, the Word of God concerning Enoch, a man who walked with God and before this translation had this testimony—that he pleased God. In the Book of Jude, verse 14, he pleased God by talking about the coming of the Lord with ten thousand of His saints. When I compare the experiences of Noah with Matthew 24; when I study the life of David; when I look at Ezekiel, Daniel, Matthew 13, Mark, Luke, and John; when I study Peter and Paul—I'm convinced that this old world will be saturated with sin when Jesus comes, and the only hope of the world is and always has been the coming of Jesus.

What shall we do about it? There's only one thing we

can do and that's to go back to the old landmarks,
namely, the sovereignty of the local church, the independence of the pulpit, the authority of the Word of God, the
centrality of the Cross, the necessity of the new birth,
separation and purity through the blessed hope—the
return of the Lord, and Bible and personal evangelism—knocking on doors, praying in people's homes,
witnessing and winning the lost to Christ.

Then we need to make some vows, and keep them. It
may cost us to make and keep a real vow, but God will
honor it, and victory will be ours through Christ Jesus.

I do not base my fellowship on just premillennial
preaching or truth, but neither would I be willing to base
it on organization or a brand. After all, brethren, the
rapture is going to bring about a mighty split one of these
days.

I do not believe in a split rapture, but I do believe a
split before the rapture would help. Now, if this is my
swan song, let me sing the amen too. With all my heart I
believe I've preached the truth. May God bless it as He
sees fit.

23

The Three "F's"

Lester's health problems continued into our marriage despite my high resolve to help him regain his health. It wasn't until he was well into his thirties that he made the discoveries that completely altered his health. He then said there were three "F's" which, if followed, could revolutionize one's life.

The first "F"—faith—was well known by his radio audience and those who heard him preach. Over and over through the years he has said, "Now the just shall live by faith," and he has practiced it. Four times—in Habakkuk, Romans, Galatians, and Hebrews—we are reminded of this. He calls Hebrews 10:32-12:4 the Pike's Peak of the Bible.

There was a second "F" he found in the Bible that he began to practice. It became a tremendous truth that he could not neglect. Jesus said, "Then shall they fast" (Mark 2:20; Luke 5:35). Moses, Elijah, and Jesus fasted forty days, thereby representing the law, the prophets, and grace. When the truth of this got hold of Lester, like any other Bible truth that became real to him, he grabbed onto it and didn't let go. "Fasting isn't an ordinance or a church doctrine," he said, "but just plain Bible truth and is a practice between the individual and the Lord. Like other great truths it has been abused and misused and therefore has come into bad repute. But why should we leave out a practice that has such a prominent place in the Scripture?" Bible in hand, he proceeded to explore this practice.

Every great revival in the Bible was preceded by fasting. The walls of Jerusalem were rebuilt after Nehemiah wept, mourned, fasted, and prayed before the God of heaven (Neh. 1:4). Fasting played an important part in the deliverance of Esther and her people with godly old Mordecai, her uncle, waiting upon the Lord for a real spiritual victory. The great Nineveh revival was preceded by the king and all of his people attiring themselves in sackcloth and going to the ash pile and there fasting and praying until God delivered the city. The message of Jonah on repentance was vital, but the reception of the message was better because they fasted and humbled themselves before the Lord.

The one book that has astounded every prophetic preacher is the book of Daniel. The wisdom of Daniel and his power are so amazing; yet in chapter 9, verse 3, we find the secret of it. "And I set my face unto the Lord God, to seek by prayer and supplications, with fasting, and sackcloth, and ashes."

Look at that mighty revival book of Joel—with its stirring call to repentance and the announcement of impending doom—calling the people to fast.

I believe the great Pentecostal revival took place after ten days of fasting and prayer. The great missionary program was launched after fasting and prayer (Acts 13:2,3). Anna served God with fastings (Luke 2:37). Paul and the mariners, as recorded in Acts 27, fasted fourteen days. In 2 Corinthians 11:27 we hear Paul say, ". . . In fastings often . . ." The Psalmist said, ". . . I humbled my soul with fastings . . ." (Ps. 35:13).

Jesus warns us concerning some things in connection with fasting. First, we are to be sincere. It's not to be a matter to show off about. Second, we are to fast unto the

Lord and not unto men. A third thing He taught us is that fasting in itself is not the reward but instead that which God gives us because of our humility and sincere desire for spiritual things. Another thing Jesus taught us is that prayer goes with fasting.

Fasting is not a way to put pressure on God to force Him to give us what we want or need, but fasting is a willingness on our part to receive gratefully what He wants to give as He supplies our needs. Fasting does not affect God, but it does affect us. Fasting does not prepare God because He is already prepared.

The first benefit to be derived must be spiritual. It will clear the channel between God and us. It will pick up the line between God's office and ours. It will patch the broken tape on our spiritual tape recorder. It will take us from among the doubters and put us among the shouters. It will keep us from being professional and mechanical in our Bible study and ministry. It will give us real compassion for the lost, the suffering, and the backslidden. It will give spiritual wisdom in the decisions we must make. The will of God will be delightful. There will be increased power in our prayer life, and our testimony will become more effective. It will clear the mind and make us more alert; it will make it easier to have the mind of Christ. It will help us to memorize and retain the Scriptures.

Many headaches are caused by surfeit and gluttony, which bring about a toxic condition because of food and saturation. Physically, fasting is a must for good health. "Fasting will impair my health," some will cry. No, the thing that has impaired your health is food—too much and the wrong kind. God will bless the practice of any truth in the Word of God, and fasting is a Bible truth.

Lester challenged our church to fast many times. It became a regular weekly practice to fast one day a week and give the price of three meals to missions. The time it would have taken to cook and eat the three meals was given to the reading of the Word of God and prayer. The fellowship of our church became richer, sweeter, and deeper. Faith was increased, missionaries were helped and blessed, and we saw many people come to the Lord as God honored another truth from His Word.

Jesus said, ". . . I am come that they might have life, and that they might have it more abundantly" (John 10:10). My husband emphasized that the Bible is a complete book; therefore, it does not leave out any of the essentials to a full and abundant life. The first "F"—faith—has to do with our spiritual salvation; the other two have to do with our fullness of living and our helpfulness to others.

Lester came to some practical conclusions regarding the third "F"—food. He became convinced that four things are killing the American people—too much food, bad food, wrong combinations of food, and anxiety and worry, which stem from an absence of faith, truth, and wisdom from God.

The doctors removed my tonsils and my appendix and treated me for stomach ulcers. Yet they remained baffled concerning some of the sick spells I had. Strange as it may seem, there wasn't but one thing ever wrong with me, and that was improper food or the wrong combinations of foods.

Daniel purposed in his heart not to defile himself, first of all, by eating the wrong things and then by drinking (Dan. 1:8). The wise man said in Proverbs 23:21, "For the drunkard and the glutton shall come to poverty...." In that verse the glutton—the man who eats too much—is yoked with the drunkard.

The Psalmist said that man is wonderfully and fearfully made. Man has never made a machine with a motor that would run 969 years like the heart of Methuselah. The human body is the only machine that can repair itself if given the proper cooperation. Man is not a mechanical machine, but a living organism, and he has innate wisdom that no other part of God's creation has been able to exercise.

Physically, you can only be what you eat or at least what you assimilate and use of that which goes into your body. . . . Who started the idea of three meals a day? Most people feel they are religiously bound to eat three square meals a day, with coffee breaks and all sorts of supplements in between. God fed Elijah only twice a day, and it probably wasn't too much of a ration because it was brought by a raven, which, of course, wouldn't have had a big baggage compartment. And yet Elijah, a specimen of tremendous physical health, could outrun the king's horses.

Find out what your body needs, and then in spite of the cost and criticism, stay with it to live longer and stronger.

For thirty-five years I lived (or rather died) on potatoes, meat, gravy, and refined sweets. . . . I turned down the fresh lettuce, the green beans, the English peas, and many other delightful and healthful things that came straight out of our garden. As a result, I was the sickest boy of the three in our family, and I baffled the doctors and was treated for everything except the right thing, namely, an improper diet.

Now don't get the idea that I am suggesting that you starve yourself to death or go on some unhappy diet.

Since he made these discoveries, my husband's diet has consisted for the most part of natural foods.

Return to the simple things like God gives them. Even though we are all aware of the fact that man has poisoned the water system and polluted the air, I still believe, in spite of the terrible conditions upon us, that with the right effort man can have a large measure of health. The food situation is like the gospel. It has been decorated, advertised, and glamorized; and at the same time it has been refined and "delifed." It looks good, tastes good, and lasts longer without spoiling. . . .

The stove is the murderer in your house. After our foods are poisoned, killed, cooked, fried, baked, boiled, stewed, mashed, hashed, and seasoned, we don't get much of the original good that was in them when they were harvested. It would be a wonderful start for you to take one day a week just to fast, and if necessary, drink a little unsweetened fruit juice or eat a piece of fruit. The body is about ninety percent liquid and therefore ought to have a lot of liquids, but liquids of the right kind.

Years ago Lester gave up drinking coffee, tea, and soft drinks. When people would ask him if he didn't like them, he'd reply, "Why, of course, I like them, and at one time I indulged in all of those things. But let me remind you that it was back in my sick days. I'm interested in being healthy because of the call of God upon my life; there's no demand for a sick body."

Who could argue with that kind of logic? I couldn't, and I certainly didn't. The things that proved helpful to him he was willing to share. "I believe we ought to eat to live," he would say, "instead of live to eat."

Can't you see the practical side of what I'm talking about? Sickness is no accident; neither is health. Sickness is an accumulation of poisons that the system could not get rid of. God has put every cleanser and purifier and eradicator in the human system that is necessary, but because of man's misuses and abuses, he makes himself sick. Your health is invaluable. It ought to be measured in terms of souls and spiritual usefulness. My body is the temple of the Holy Spirit and must be attended to according to His good pleasure.

I have gotten away from white sugar, white flour, an abundance of meat, and milk, which is mucous-forming and causes congestion in my system bringing on sore throats and colds.

I begin my day with a great big juicy verse or a chapter of the Word of God and then, before reading a number of chapters and entering into a season of prayer, I usually drink a big glass of grapefruit juice. If I cannot get grapefruit juice, I drink a big glass of lime or lemon water. If no juice is available, I will drink just a big glass of water.

For breakfast sometimes I will have chopped dates, figs, raisins, a banana, a piece of whole wheat toast or other good whole grain bread and honey, along with some nuts or sunflower seed sprinkled over the fruit. Or I may have a bowl of steel-cut oats or whole-grain cereal or other health food cereal that still has the life in it. Many times I have grapes, pears, apples, or fresh peaches with nuts. Or I may have dried apples or apricots (properly soaked), mixed with some cashew butter (or almond butter and honey), and topped with nuts and various seeds—what a delicious breakfast! And occasionally, if I eat eggs, I either eat the yolks after steaming them slowly in butter in a covered pan, or have them poached. With the eggs I eat whole grain toast and honey, or toast and Fig Pep, which is a product made from black mission figs. During fruit season I may have a cantaloupe or watermelon. Sometimes I put a little cream, or preferably goat's milk, over my cereal and over the dates, figs, and raisins. Raw milk, of course, is better because it still has the culture and the life.

Lester spends much time in travel. He carries with him these types of foods and has remained a youthful, vibrantly healthy man. When questioned (and at times teased in a somewhat mocking way), he responds, "Friend, it's just a matter of whether or not you want to be well."

Something that has amazed us is how little he can eat and still feel good and go as hard as he does. Many people have said to him, "I don't understand how you can have so many ministries, go so many miles, preach so many times, and yet stay alive."

His answer has been, "Let me be quick to say that the first secret is the goodness of God and faith in Him and His Word. But on the human side, He certainly has blessed the efforts we have put forth in temple care." He was referring, of course, to his body which the Bible calls the temple of the Holy Spirit.

In addition to urging people to eat food in its raw state for maximum health, he cautions about proper utensils for food preparation (discard aluminum pans and invest in stainless steel). Our kitchen is equipped with a vegetable juicer and a blender. If homemakers find it difficult to get away from cooking food, he urges them to use very little water, keep the pan tightly closed, and cook just until tender.

He is also an advocate of bodily exercise; "You'd be surprised to know what a brisk walk of at least a mile every day with the proper deep breathing will do for you. Much of the body is dead because of a lack of exercise," Lester says.

These things (and much more) he shared through the pages of the monthly publication, *Faith Enterprise*, and also in a small book entitled *Food, Fasting and Faith.*

We both know that, along with an increased faith in God, the reason he is still active in the ministry today is that the Lord has graciously showed him and taught him these things.

I came to the place where I was physically depleted and disturbed, and even though I was stubborn to begin with, God laid it on my heart to learn these lessons. . . .

I enjoy eating now more than I ever did before because of the simple truths that the Lord has taught me—much of it through friends who have been so kind. You mothers owe it to your children to build strong bodies that will resist disease.

The Bible says that food is sanctified by the Word of God and prayer. Surely we believe in praying over our food, but we ought to also believe in praying over the right kind and the right amount, eaten under the right conditions. We need happiness and sweet fellowship at mealtimes in our homes in order for our systems to do their best with what we consume.

The beloved apostle John said, "Beloved, I wish above all things that thou mayest prosper and be in health, even as thy soul prospereth" (3 John 2). And Paul wrote, "And the very God of peace sanctify you wholly; and I pray God your whole spirit and soul and body be preserved blameless unto the coming of our Lord Jesus Christ. Faithful is He that calleth you, who also will do it" (1 Thess. 5:23,24).

What a blessing from heaven to have good health in order that we might win more souls to Christ and witness with more power. Here's a Scripture that covers it all: "Whether therefore ye eat, or drink, or whatsoever ye do, do all to the glory of God" (1 Cor. 10:31).

24

A Work of Faith for Forgotten Men

"We do not base our ministry on the worthiness of the one in need but on our love for Christ."

Such was the motivation that propelled my husband into the ministry of reaching out to those the world calls "undesirables." In time this work would be named the "City of Refuge."

"The milk of human kindness will never leave the breast of the redeemed child of God," Lester said as he viewed the desperate plight of those caught in the clutches of sin. He determined to do something about society's outcasts.

The Good Samaritan Rescue Mission had been taken under the wings of our Alameda Baptist Church (with the dedicated superintendency of Tom Murphrey, who had been converted listening to the Family Altar Program), and a second Good Samaritan had been opened in Big Spring, Texas. It was a wonderful, God-blessed work, but my husband's heart ached as he saw the limited way in which the men who came to the missions were helped. They were fed, given a place to sleep, preached to, and given whatever help the missions could provide. And then they were gone. "Please pray for this great work," Lester pleaded both to the church and to his radio audience. "Surely this kind of work was close to the heart of Jesus as he ate with the publicans and sinners and said, 'I came not to call the righteous, but sinners to repentance.' "

The slogan for the work became "A work of faith for forgotten men."

The rescue missions were a wonderful ministry, but the feeling persisted that the men who came there needed more permanent help. Lester began to get a burden for a place for the men to go after they left the missions. In Ephesians 5:16 and Colossians 4:5, we are told to "redeem" the time. Actually, this means "buy it up."

Referring to Genesis 18:14, Lester said to me, "Is anything too hard for the Lord?" I knew what that meant: he was girding himself for action.

Before I knew it, Lester was talking about "a modern miracle—the 'City of Refuge.' " Never before had he begun a project that so captured the confidence of people and stirred the interest of multitudes. In February, 1957, Mr. and Mrs. Arnold Jensen gave to the Roloff Evangelistic Enterprises eighty acres of land six miles west of Lexington, Texas. The property was without fences, wells for water, electricity, or buildings. Lester looked at it, and God gave the vision of what it could become.

On its first anniversary he shared with the radio audience:

With a conviction as deep as life itself that we were to rescue the perishing, care for the dying, and snatch them in pity from sin and the grave, we started out.

We have bought seven house trailers and erected a quonset hut given by Dr. and Mrs. Logan of Corpus Christi. The water well was dug by Bill Sipes, Clyde Dodd, and J. V. Biggs. A nice barn was built by Mr. King, one of the men who had come to the City of Refuge, and fences have been erected, land has been cleared, and one crop has been harvested. An orchard has been started, and also a herd of goats and a herd of cattle have been started. Counting the two rescue missions, almost fifty thousand meals have been served. Clothes and shelter have been furnished for many people. A big brick building, forty feet wide and one hundred feet long, is being finished now. A two-ton truck, a pickup, and a station wagon have been purchased along with many minor items. All of this, which represents a value of at least $150,000, has been done for $42,500.

The Austin, Texas, newspaper devoted a page to photos and an article telling of the work. The report was entitled "The Seventh City of Refuge." Lester had told them of the six biblical cities of refuge. In the Old Testament, when people were in trouble, they could go to these cities of refuge and hide until their difficulties could be straightened out. In the February, 1958, edition of the *Faith Enterprise*, he wrote:

Dear Friend, if we would have had any doubt about the need for the City of Refuge a year ago, that doubt has long since been settled. We've been able to help many people already, homes have gone back together, little children have had the privilege of living normal lives and doing good school work. The school bus comes to the door of the City of Refuge every morning, and we hope eventually to have our own school. We have had inquiries from a thousand or more people who need to be at the City of Refuge.

In Proverbs 11:24,25, "There is that scattereth, and yet increaseth; and there is that withholdeth more than is meet, but it tendeth to poverty. The liberal souls shall be made fat: and he that watereth shall be watered also himself." Proverbs 13:7: "There is that maketh himself rich, yet hath nothing; there is that maketh himself poor, yet hath great riches." Proverbs 17:5: "Whoso mocketh the poor reproacheth his Maker . . . ." Proverbs 19:17: "He that hath pity upon the poor lendeth unto the Lord; and that which he hath given will he pay him again." Proverbs 21:13: "Whoso stoppeth his ears at the cry of the poor, he also shall cry himself, but shall not be heard." Proverbs 28:27: "He that giveth unto the poor shall not lack: but he that hideth his eyes shall have many a curse."

In 1958 Lester read figures which said seven million alcoholics in this country needed help. He received thousands of letters from alcoholics, their families, and penitentiary inmates begging for help. He told radio listeners:

The state has built tuberculosis hospitals, crippled children's hospitals, and other kinds of hospitals, yet there has been no real provision made for spiritual "lepers" and those who have been crippled by sin. As I have driven to the City of Refuge with as many as five men in the car, they would look up and see on Highway 112 the big sign saying "City of Refuge," and their faces would lighten and their conversation would brighten as they looked forward to this city of hope where they could begin to live again. I'm not saying we help everyone; some refuse the gospel and refuse to accept the deliverance that the Lord Jesus offers. We are able to help only those who really want to be helped. But there is no need for failure at the City of Refuge.

Many had questions about the "city"—its needs, its mode

of operation, and its future. We did not know, of course, that in the years ahead many such faith enterprises would be started by my husband, and that like-minded people would be willing to come and staff these places. But Lester's answers to the questions now are basically the same answers he gave more than twenty years ago.

Who may go to the City of Refuge?

Anyone who has a real need for help or anybody who wants to go and be a helper.

What does one do to get into the City of Refuge?

Simply write a letter, agree to stay at least ninety days, and cooperate fully when you come.

What does it cost?

Not one penny. If people have money they want to share, they just give it to the Enterprises, which is responsible for the City of Refuge and the rescue missions.

Do you have a place for old people?

For years Lester had to answer in the negative, but today that is not true, as you will discover in chapter 23.

How do you go about providing buildings at the "city"?

This is a work of faith, entirely dependent upon the gifts of God's people. You talk about an opportunity for evangelism! This is it, when we have men, women, boys, and girls for at least ninety days to preach the gospel of deliverance to them. Some have suggested that we appeal to the state for funds, but this is a work of faith and there must be no strings attached that would keep us from preaching a full gospel and ministering to the spiritual needs of people. This is not a social institution. This is a salvation institution.

What are the needs at the City of Refuge?

That is easy to answer. We need food, clothes, linens, bed covers, wash towels, razor blades, toothpaste, toothbrushes, furniture, and feed for the cattle, goats, chickens, and turkeys. But, oh, the cry of my heart is for buildings and a place to put the people who need to come.

As Lester appealed for help for this great ministry, he said:

Let's listen to the Savior, the One who gave two-thirds of His life taking care of the poor and the needy, the One who suffered great persecution and misunderstanding because He ate with publicans and sinners. His answer to the accusations was, "They that are whole need not a physician: but they that are sick. . . . I came not to call the righteous, but sinners to repentance. . . . The Son of man came not to be ministered unto, but to minister, and to give his life a ransom for many. . . . For ye have the poor always with you."

To assure John that He was the Messiah, Jesus sent a messenger saying, "to the poor the gospel is preached." Jesus, in Luke 10, let the lawyer know that the man who is ditched but not dead needs to be cared for, and the man who shows mercy upon the poor and the needy is the good neighbor. The wise man said, "He that hath pity on the poor lendeth to the Lord." He also said if we stop our ears at the cry of the poor, we will stop the answer to our prayers. The City of Refuge is not a flop farm for bums and ne'er-do-wells but for angels off the trail.

The "city with a soul," as some chose to call the work, received unprecedented response from across America. People were coming and writing from everywhere in desperate need for spiritual help. Lester wrote concerned friends:

We need the power of God, more love, and compassion

137

for those who have been branded helpless and hopeless. Only the power of the gospel of Jesus Christ can save and deliver those who've staggered and slobbered from one jailhouse to another, from one pen to another, and from one alcoholic institution to another. Apart from the power of God, we might as well close down. So please pray—I say, please pray for the City of Refuge. It will fail as we fail to pray and trust God for the supernatural power of the Holy Spirit.

To me, the "city" is Christianity with its work clothes on. It's Jesus at the well-curb. It's Jesus breaking up a stoning party and saying, "Go and sin no more." It's Jesus on the Cross, saying to an old and bloody, hell-bound thief, "Today shalt thou be with me in paradise." It's Paul and Silas in the Philippian jail at midnight saying, "Do thyself no harm: for we are all here. . . . Believe on the Lord Jesus Christ, and thou shalt be saved."

25

Our Need Is "Kneeology"

The work of evangelism continued with Lester spending many lonely days and nights away from us and the church. There were times when he fulfilled as many as fifty engagements in three states in a short period of time. Always the big thirty-two-foot gospel van would come back loaded with gifts for the City of Refuge. Help for the "city" continued to pour in, not only in cash gifts, but sometimes in unexpected ways.

The Alameda Baptist Church family was loyal and loving. In every way they were tremendously supportive, and revival fires continued to burn brightly. "We're trying to hold the torch high for freedom and liberty in the building of a New Testament church that's geared for evangelism," my husband explained.

The work of the Park Avenue Christian Day School, the operation of two Rescue Missions and the City of Refuge, the production of the Family Altar radio broadcast, the publication of the *Faith Enterprise*, the needs of the church family—all of this was more than enough work and responsibility for one man. No wonder he wrote in 1960 that his heart was burdened and troubled.

The very desperation of this hour, the destitution of our world, the black clouds of destiny, and the impending judgment and doom that hang over this Christ-rejecting, God-defying, and Bible-denying world is enough to drive us to our knees.

We've emphasized psychology, sociology, theology, but our need is "kneeology." Therefore, we've called our workers in our ministry to their knees for the Word of God and prayer every day at noon. And we are setting the last Thursday in every month as a day of fasting and praying. . . .

The devil and some friends have tried to convince us we've tried to do too much with too little, but I must affirm one more time that faith always must run ahead of sight. . . .

When nothing whereon to lean remains,
When strongholds crumble to dust,
When nothing is sure but that God still reigns,
That's just the time to trust.
'Tis better to walk by faith than sight
In this path of yours and mine,
In the pitch black night with no outer light,
That's the time for faith to shine.

With the Bible in our hands we have only the promises of God's provisions, but we believe that that is sufficient. Hospitals, reform schools, and penitentiaries are not the answer. At the City of Refuge we present a faithful Christ for failing men. Jesus stood on the shore near the fishermen's failure and said, "Launch out into the deep, and let down your nets for a draught." To which they said, "We have toiled all the night, and have taken nothing: nevertheless at thy word . . . ." And my friends, the Word brought faith and fish.

A precious friend who used to be an enemy of the cross and of our ministry stood in our church to give a marvelous testimony and began it by saying, "The Lord saved my soul and gave me a fishing pole."

By the great grace and mercy of God, testimonies like that became more and more frequent as word filtered back to us about men, women, and children who had surrendered their lives to the Lord. "Kneeology" and its role in the Roloff ministries could never be denied. When Lester began the first City of Refuge, he asked God to give him just one man that was completely delivered and transformed. God has answered that prayer many times over, but the first one was Victor Edge, who later became a preacher of the gospel. Many men left the "city" and enrolled in Bible schools. Later they went on to Tennessee Temple College, graduated, and entered full-time evangelistic, missionary, or pastoral work. We long ago lost count of the numbers of men and women in ministries such as this.

More buildings were needed at the City of Refuge, and radio listeners were alerted. A Houston friend of the radio ministry invited my husband to call. She invited him into her little old-fashioned house and asked him to tell her more about the "city." After she was thoroughly convinced that he was the radio preacher, she took an old walking stick, reached under a table, pulled out a paper sack, and said, "Hold out your hand." She then put a thousand-dollar bill into Lester's hand. She proceeded to give him another thousand-dollar bill, another, and another—and then two five-hundred dollar bills and two one-hundred dollar bills. She said, "I may need to move to the 'city' sometime, and I will need something firm to stand on." Earlier God had told my husband that the foundation to the next building would be taken care of, and he recognized as the woman spoke that God was confirming that promise.

141

26

The Lighthouse for Boys

Lonely, lonely, lonely is the Intracoastal Canal forty miles from Corpus Christi.

The waters are stirred by an occasional towboat and barge, a few commercial and sport fishermen.

The restless Gulf of Mexico is out of sight behind dune-barricaded Padre Island. The only change winter brings is a shallow sheen of tide, covering the bleak flats, or swirling sand when a norther blows the cold weather tides out into the Gulf.

Such was the description *Houston Chronicle* reporter Melvin Steakley gave in September, 1964, of the setting for the Lighthouse for Boys, another Enterprises' work of faith that Lester felt burdened to begin.

This work was started in the summer of 1958 to provide a place for delinquent boys to be isolated from drugs and liquor until they were delivered. The Lighthouse houseboat was built by Brother E. A. Goodman. The true stories to come out of the Lighthouse work would fill a book by themselves. In the early days of this ministry we took in boys as young as age nine. After our initial bout with the welfare department and the state of Texas, we had to set the age limit at seventeen. The Lighthouse has been a haven for boys no one else wanted—boys who were one step from reform school or the penitentiary.

Visitors to this work either have to be flown in or go in

by boat. Its inaccessibility has made it impossible for those who are sent there for help to walk or swim out. When the *Houston Chronicle* reporter went in to photograph the boys and to report on the work, his reaction mirrored the feelings of others who go there from time to time. My husband, of course, goes there frequently, but he has entrusted the overseeing of the boys to others, just as he has in the other ministries.

The boys come in all sizes and shapes, but they have one thing in common regardless of their age—they are old in sorrow, sadness, and hostility. It has been amazing to watch such a mixture of humanity—the boys from the southern states with their twang, the boys from the city slums with the incorrect grammar, and the boys from the affluent suburbs who speak precisely.

At first the boys cover their inward hurts with belligerence and a bravado that they do not actually possess. These boys are almost without exception bereft of parental love and guidance. Some are actually homeless while others have rebelled against parental authority and have gotten into serious trouble with the law. In its first seven years of the ministry, my husband recorded almost six hundred boys who found their first real home at the Lighthouse.

The Lighthouse facilities in and of themselves would be considered austere—the bunkhouse, the mess hall, the little outlying shanties, and the houseboat itself. But the love they receive and the camaraderie that develops more than make up for any lack of creature comforts. The food has always been plentiful and nourishing.

The Lighthouse accommodates from twenty to twenty-five boys at any one time. They are kept busy fishing, working in the garden, and reading the Bible. Life for these boys becomes a blend of horseplay, work, and fun. But there is strict discipline. Rules are meant to be obeyed; these are boys who have broken the rules and laws laid down by society—they have raped, stolen, and attempted murder. Many of them are runaways. There can be no coddling at the Lighthouse. The Bible says the way of the transgressor is hard—regardless of one's age.

The Lighthouse offers a haven, and more important it gives the boys an opportunity for a new way of life. Here many have their first introduction to Jesus Christ. They learn that God loves them and that He has given rules of conduct in His Word that, when followed, result in harmonious living and a deep inner peace. Much time is devoted to Bible study, and there is memorization of such portions of Scripture as Psalms 1, 23, 91, 100, and 121; 1 John 1; Isaiah 40:28-31; and 1 Corinthians 13.

Ever since the Lighthouse work began, fishing has played an important role, not only in keeping the boys busy, but also from the standpoint of practicality. Fish have always been abundant in the intracoastal waters. During the summer months, the nighttime crews catch anywhere from two hundred to six hundred pounds of speckled trout. Trout lines are also run during daylight hours.

This much fish requires many man-hours of cleaning and filleting. Fish is an important part of the diet not only at the Lighthouse, but at all of the Roloff Enterprises' homes. Some of the fish is sold through commercial channels when our own freezers are full.

Ronnie Doring, was taken to the Lighthouse. He later became one of our leaders. On the occasion of my husband's birthday he wrote a letter to the *Faith Enterprise Newsletter* in which he told of coming to the Lighthouse in 1968.

After a long trip by boat down the Intracoastal Canal, we finally arrived. My first reaction was, "Well, where is the lighthouse?" Like almost everybody else, I expected to see a tall tower and a big rotating beacon. No, there is no lighthouse like that at the Lighthouse.

The Lighthouse itself is a simple and rugged place. In 1969 I returned once more. I had never in my life seen anything like the Christian spirit that was there. I was saved early that summer and remained for the rest of the summer and part of the next summer in 1970.

Ronnie worked for a construction outfit in Corpus Christi for awhile and then felt God was calling him to spend time working at the Lighthouse as a leader. He called the time spent doing that "the most rewarding of my life." Of my husband he wrote, "I have been acquainted with Brother Roloff since 1968. I have never received a greater blessing from any one man in my life. I was saved under his ministry—I have watched that ministry grow and it has watched me grow. By faith in the Word of God and prayer, both the workers and the work continue to grow."

One of the things that has thrilled my husband most has been watching these boys become born-again believers—individuals capable of returning to society as whole men who are able to make a worthy life for themselves and contribute to the betterment of the world. As my husband goes to campuses such as Bob Jones University, Tennessee Temple, and others, he finds boys who have been at the Lighthouse and who are now studying for the ministry in order to go out and serve the Lord. When he sees them, Lester stops in awe and says with gratitude, "Had it not been for the Lighthouse, they would either be dead or in prison today."

The *Houston Chronicle* reporter (mentioned at the outset of this chapter) concluded his pictorial survey of the Lighthouse work by stating:

Upon graduation from the Lighthouse and the "City of Refuge," many of the boys set out to "make a preacher," living by the Bible and eschewing tobacco, alcohol, narcotics, dancing, and mixed swimming, even the very appearance of sin.

The simple morality, often couched largely in negative terms, is warmed, sweetened, and ennobled by a compassion for others who stagger and stumble under the burden of a broken home, parents who love alcohol more than their children, and the terrifying loneliness which is the lot of the unloved.

These "preacher boys" were turned aside from the reform school and a life of crime by this view which looks at good and evil in black and white. Their conviction that they have something to share will put evangelistic fervor into pulpits across the nation for many years to come.

From the Lighthouse's beginning, hundreds of boys have come from lives of drugs and crime. In more recent years the Lighthouse has taken in young men who have already received sentences in penitentiaries. As word has gotten out about the miraculous changes in the lives of these young men, judges across the country have granted young men probationary sentences and allowed them to come to us where, as my husband says, 2 Corinthians 5:17 has become a reality in their lives: "Therefore if any man be in Christ, he is a new creature: old things are passed away; behold, all things are become new."

Some people are shocked when they learn that, during the last several years of the Lighthouse ministry, if the prison terms each boy faced at that time were added together, they would amount to more than two hundred years. But it is equally true that some of the finest preachers across our land today are products of the Lighthouse ministry—men who were saved by God's marvelous grace and called to preach the Word of God.

In the summer of 1977 at the yearly "Camp Meeting" in Culloden, Georgia, my husband told the story of Bruce Quinn from Dalton, Georgia, who tried to run away from the Lighthouse. After walking all night and the next day across marshland, wire grass, sand, and salt water, Bruce panicked and almost gave up. He lay down in some water and then got up and started walking again. He stumbled across an old, deserted, red-and-white truck between Laguna Madre and the Gulf of Mexico. He got in the truck, which had a C.B. radio that was still workable, got on the microphone and hollered, "HELP!"

Many miles away a lady heard him, and he told her, "Tell Brother Roloff to get in the plane and come look for me." It was almost dark, and my husband was due to preach in forty minutes, but he ran to the airport hangar and flew down the island. Miraculously, he saw the desperate lad. Lester found a little trail of a road to land on and picked him up. My husband says:

I think that experience convinced this young man of two things—that God really loved him and so did we. He has been a fine boy ever since. He knew that I risked my life to save his. But, oh, there is a sweeter story than this. Jesus gave His life, and I hope you will hear the cry of His blood from that old Roman cross saying, "Come unto me, all ye that labor and are heavy laden, and I will give you rest."

Sinner friend, trust Him today. Christian, tell others that the blood of Jesus Christ, God's Son, still cleanses us from all sin. Get on your spiritual C.B. and holler, "HELP!" and Heaven will dispatch the angel of mercy, even as the song writer said, "He saw me plunged in deep distress and flew to my relief. For me He bore that shameful cross and carried all my grief."

Remember, *today* is the day of salvation and *now* is the time.

27

Airborne

Never has the keeping power of God been more evident in the work of Roloff Evangelistic Enterprises than in the many varied experiences Lester has had in flying. When he talks about these brushes with death, he says, "My only explanation for still being alive is that many, many wonderful people have prayed for me constantly." He was determined to learn to fly—whatever the cost. "I never paid any price like the price I've paid for flying," he admits. "When we are seeking to get His message out, God will go a long way to protect the one that bears it and delivers it." In my husband's case God has some angelic helpers who have been mighty overworked!

At one time Lester spent a tremendous amount of time getting from one place to another. He had a passionate dislike for flying, probably the result of some earlier unfortunate experiences while flying in little cracker-box planes in several emergency situations. When he tells about them now, he makes them sound hilarious, but at the time he honestly thought he was going to die.

His maiden flight was in a little Piper Cub. He had to get to Corsicana, Texas, in a hurry to preach the funeral service for his brother's mother-in-law. That day he was wearing a beautiful new hat the members of the church had given him. The plane made it to Austin, and the pilot said they would have to go down for gas. Lester felt he was "sick unto death" and just lay there. He had the plane window open, and out went his new hat. "It didn't bother me," he says, "because I didn't think I would live too long, and they wouldn't bury me in a hat anyway!"

They never did make it to Corsicana in time for the funeral. "It was dark when we landed," he explains. "The sun had gone down, and I had serious doubts I would ever see it come up again."

His second experience in flying was not much better. Later he said, "When I get home to heaven, the first person I want to see after I see Jesus is my old, tired guardian angel. I want to take him some vitamins and carrot juice!"

So it was a distinct shock to all of us who were familiar with Lester's airsickness when he finally decided he would have to learn to fly in order to conserve time in getting from one place to another. The flying lessons began in 1958. It was Roger and Elaine Gault who finally convinced him he could do it. Typically, Lester said to Roger, "Well, I'll have to have a Scripture. I can't fly unless I fly scripturally."

Isaiah 40:28-31 reinforced Lester's decision to become an airborne messenger of the gospel:

Hast thou not known? hast thou not heard, that the everlasting God, the Lord, the Creator of the ends of the earth, fainteth not, neither is weary? there is no searching of his understanding. He giveth power to the faint; and to them that have no might he increaseth strength.

Even the youths shall faint and be weary, and the young men shall utterly fall:

But they that wait upon the Lord shall renew their strength; they shall mount up with wings as eagles; they shall run, and not be weary; and they shall walk, and not faint.

"That is the verse I felt gave me permission to start flying," he explains. "I began thirteen of the most dangerous years I have ever lived. I have had to ask the Lord to forgive me for the foolish moments and the days and nights of flying when I ought to have been on the ground, but I always thought I had to get somewhere to preach. All my flying has been wrapped around people. God has been so faithful because He knows that, in spite of my foolishness, ignorance, and carelessness, I have been on my way with the Bible, and He knew when I landed I was going to preach or help someone find his way to Him. It is simply a matter of getting out the gospel. That is why I fly."

Roger Gault, his first instructor, had to be patient, and I am sure he had many misgivings about whether Lester would ever make a pilot. There were a number of others—people like Harold Cadd and Norman Martin—who worked with him before he finally made it.

He has landed twice with a dead engine; he has landed four times in a twin-engine plane with only one engine running. He landed one time at midnight on a highway and crossed under two sets of power lines before bringing the plane to a safe stop. Twice he has landed on freeways. He has been in hail storms and weather where he has feared for his life, but through it all the Lord has brought him safely to his destination.

He describes some of those experiences in more detail:

We were flying along at 10,500 feet, and the trim-tab push rod on a part of the elevator came apart, bringing about a tremendous vibration that made it difficult to hold the controls. Morgan Parris, my faithful helper and co-pilot, was with me. It was about ten at night. We declared an emergency with the Atlanta Center. They told us where the closest airport was, and we headed in that direction. A military jet pilot heard of our difficulty and volunteered his help . . . we thought the "Queen Air" would shake itself to pieces. In a matter of moments the jet pilot had come to our side and was talking with us. He said, "I'm just off of your right wing, and I will guide you to the airport." We had to make three 360 degree turns in order to come down and make a safe approach. Just before we landed at this old deserted military airport, the jet pilot said, "I'm going to make a low pass and make sure there are no cows on the runway." We whispered our gratitude to this unknown friend while he went on his way. Even so, many have been the times when the Lord has whispered to us in our faith-flights through this wonderful ministry, "I'm just off of your right wing, and I'll guide you safely in."

Our family went through much agony until Lester finished his flight tests, earned his wings, and became a pilot. The Lord kept telling him, "Son, why don't you use your instruments when you fly?" and Lester had to admit he wasn't qualified to do so. With his usual determination he set about to master instrument flying as well. Lester admits that he has never been much afraid of anything, but getting his instrument ticket just about did him in. When it came time for his check ride to determine if he had finally qualified (after several previous failures), he came out of it with the white ticket he had been working so long for. "It was a sweet and blessed time," he explains. "Tears flowed, and I raised my hands and started praising the Lord. God is faithful!"

As is to be expected, Lester sees a spiritual analogy in his flying-lesson experiences.

It does not matter who you are; one of these days Jesus is going to say, "It is time for your check ride." I might have flunked three check rides, but there is one check ride I am not going to flunk. God is going to say one of these days, "Now you can take off your hood. You can take off that church hood, your denominational hood, your good-works hood, your money-making hood, and your religious hood. Now look at yourself as I see you." And I tell you, friend, if you flunk God's check ride, you will fall into hell. Yes, your hood will come off one of these days. You cannot fool Christ.

On that final day Jesus will say, "Take off that hood. You have been looking through a glass darkly, but now, face to face; you have known in part, but now you are going to know even as you are known." That will be the final landing, and I will be home.

When I received my white ticket and walked out of the building, I sang, "Like a bird out of prison, I have taken my flight. . . ."

28

Everlasting Arms and Eternal Wings

When Lester received his instrument pilot's license, I began to breathe easier about his flights. I knew the ATC (Air Traffic Control) could guide him better, he could come down through the clouds, and he could make instrument-guided approaches. In every way he and those flying with him would be safer. He has since flown many people to a new way of life as he has brought them to one of the homes in Georgia, Mississippi, or Texas.

There were still many close calls in the flights, but never any serious injuries nor crashes. On July 30, 1960, at the morning church service in Corpus Christi, Lester used an illustration to show that spiritual power can be given and needs met just as God delivered the ancient Israelites in many trying situations.

On the previous Saturday night, during a routine flight from Houston to Corpus Christi, the need for a manifestation of God's supernatural power had become evident. Before the flight began, the engine of the four-seat Piper plane had seemed in good form as it was revved up on the runway. Take-off was easy and the altitude gain was natural and smooth. Suddenly, while the plane was still within calling distance of the radio at International Airport in Houston, the engine began to cough, sputter, backfire, and cut out. Quickly he radioed the airport. Immediately the response came back, "Come in, 64 Zebra. The way is cleared." The tower radioed that the crippled plane had permission to land on any runway it came to. As the faltering plane headed back to Houston's airport, the three passengers prayed for deliverance. When they landed, there was quite a reception on the strip, including three fire trucks. There had been a complete and quick evacuation of other planes and equipment to clear the way. An all-out preparation for the saving of three lives was made—my husband's, his secretary's, and her husband's. Never had the earth looked sweeter nor people dearer than when they landed safely. The "Mayday!" call had been heeded. The Word of our God had prevailed, and the angels had once again delivered God's children.

On another occasion on his way to Chattanooga where the Honey Bee Quartet (from the Rebekah Home for Girls) was to sing at Tennessee Temple, he had to land on the freeway. Leave it to Lester to take advantage of the crowd that gathered in that situation! He got out his Bible and testified to the Lord's power and faithfulness. When they finally made it to the service, Dr. Lee Roberson asked him about the incident and he said, "Well, the Bible says to go out in the highways and hedges and compel them to come in."

A freak near-mishap occurred on an approach into the Memphis airport. Stan Williams was flying with him. The radio control tower's system was not working right, and they missed the approach. Visibility was very poor. Lester and Stan received another vector approach, came in, and saw the runway, but they ran into a fog bank and had to go back to instruments. About two hundred feet off the ground the twin-engine plane turned upside down, a freakish thing that should have caused them to crash. They saw the gyroscope go upside down. My husband became disoriented

155

and was pulling on the stick, and at the same time Stan was pushing on it. They looked up and saw street lights! They then gained some elevation, all the while flying upside down, and managed to get the plane right side up. They turned on the autopilot and got their breath back. They made an approach onto another runway and made it without further mishap. My husband credits Stan's knowledge of instrument flying and "the touch of an unseen Hand" for saving their lives.

One of the most serious incidents occurred in 1972 on a return trip from Florida with the Honey Bees. A fire broke out in the right engine, and an emergency landing was made. But when Lester tried to open the door, it wouldn't budge. They were trapped inside with a flaming right engine. The only way out was through the tiny window on the pilot's side, and Lester somehow managed it. Later he had the scraped sides and sore muscles around his ribs to prove it! But he was able to open the door from the outside and rescue the girls.

In all these varied experiences we have seen the everlasting arms and eternal wings of our wonderful Lord. Lester has often said that these things only make him homesick for heaven, but they have given him a greater appreciation for Psalm 121, the beloved Psalm that speaks of the great safety of the godly who put their trust in God's protection:

I will lift up mine eyes unto the hills, from whence cometh my help.

My help cometh from the Lord, which made heaven and earth.

He will not suffer thy foot to be moved: he that keepeth thee will not slumber.

Behold, he that keepeth Israel shall neither slumber nor

sleep.

The Lord is thy keeper: the Lord is thy shade upon thy right hand.

The sun shall not smite thee by day, nor the moon by night.

The Lord shall preserve thee from all evil: he shall preserve thy soul.

The Lord shall preserve thy going out and thy coming in from this time forth, and even for evermore.

What a comfort it is to know that God is the Bodyguard of His saints. And not only does He keep us, but He gives refreshment as He renews us and sends us daily on our way.

29

Take This Child

The phrase "Take this child" (Exod. 2:9) spoke to Lester's heart as the Lighthouse work continued to grow, and the need for a year-round operation of this nature made itself known in many ways.

As usual, the radio program afforded the opportunity to continually let the needs of the ministry be known to an ever-growing audience. "There is no end of what can be done for Christ if Christians will get the vision with us and help bear the burden," Lester said. "From this challenge in Exodus 2 there came a mighty deliverer called Moses. It wasn't but a little while until the Scripture says, 'Moses stood up and helped them.' After 430 years of starving bondage, millions of God's people walked across the Red Sea dryshod, out of Egyptian bondage, under the leadership of a man who was rescued when just a child. If alcoholics whose lives were redeemed at the City of Refuge are now preaching the Gospel of Christ, what will be the prospects for these precious lads who find Christ and His will if Jesus tarries?

"We must enter into this opportunity," he pleaded. "Get the picture in Exodus 2:23 of the people for whom Moses gave his life: '. . . The children of Israel sighed by reason of the bondage, and they cried, and their cry came up unto God by reason of the bondage.' As prayerfully as I know how and with emotion in my soul, I am asking God to let the cry of these children come up into your heart."

A bunkhouse and a new dining room were built at the Lighthouse facilities. Newspapers at that time were reporting that boys at a reformatory were rebelling, escaping, and killing guards. Our *Faith Enterprise* paper was able to print that our boys were responding to consistent and loving discipline. They had come to respect and recognize authority. We learned that it took as long as nine months to a year before the boys had as much stability as they needed to be ready to go out into the world once again. The helpers and leaders made all the difference in the world as they, with dedicated love, took these boys, stood by them, and helped them. Lester told supporters:

The Bible has a good deal to say about children. We have challenges in the Bible concerning lads, such as, "God heard the voice of the lad," "Arise, lift up the lad," and "God was with the lad." Abraham said, "I and the lad will go yonder," which had to do with going to worship God. "His life is bound up in the lad's life" was a statement concerning Jacob and one of his boys. "The lad knew not any thing" was a picture of the lad's innocence.

Let's look at the enemies of lads today. We are blinder than blind if we cannot and do not see that the lads of this hour have more enemies, temptations, and pitfalls than any other lads who have ever lived.

Lester has said, "Doubt says 'don't because you can't,' but faith says 'do because God is able'! In heaven there will be no lost to lead to Christ; there will be no drunkards to redeem; there will be no broken homes to put back together; there will be no wayward boys to take to the Lighthouse. All that we do for others must be done in time and not in eternity."

30

Others

As General Booth, the founder of the Salvation Army, lay on his deathbed, there was a big Salvation Army convention going on, and everyone was looking forward to a message from the old general who had started that great work. Sure enough, it came by telegram, and the message had only one word: "OTHERS."

On the occasion of the fifth anniversary of the City of Refuge, Bobby McMeens, along with his wife and two children, came to be the "city's" superintendent. It had been a difficult work from the beginning with failures as well as successes. For some time God had been speaking to my husband's heart about the necessity of moving the work to another location. My husband enjoys telling about it.

A good friend of mine, Al Gaines (whose father-in-law came to the Lord and was delivered from alcoholism under our ministry), under the pretense of taking me for a plane ride and showing me a new airplane, took me to a beautiful place. He asked me if we had any use for the P.D.T. Ranch, known formerly as the Rutherfordton Plantation, to which I replied, "None whatsoever." We landed on the runway of this beautiful estate, and as we walked around I said, "Al, this is too rich for my blood!"

On the land there was a beautiful antebellum home which had been spared from destruction during the Civil War because the lady of the home was seriously ill at the

My husband says, "All my flying has been wrapped around people. . . . It is simply a matter of getting out the gospel. That is why I fly."

My husband says: "We work with tomorrow's criminals today, but by God's grace we have seen victory in the lives of thousands of them, even rapists and murderers. We know that Christ is the Answer. . . ."
Bible study such as this is a regular and daily occurrence at the Lighthouse and in all the homes.

The Lighthouse work on the intracoastal canal.
"In heaven there will be no lost to lead to Christ; there will be no drunkards to redeem; there will be no broken homes to put back together; there will be no wayward boys to take to the Lighthouse. All that we do for others must be done in time and not in eternity."

Mrs. Smith, Superintendent, Peaceful Valley Home for retired friends of Roloff Enterprises, with fresh grown broccoli from our gardens.

For many years Lester carried a concern for our older Christian friends. So it was that in 1969 the Peaceful Valley Home became another venture of faith.

"The right kind of love would lock and stop the wheels of divorce, delinquency, murder, and war and turn this hell on earth into a haven of peace, rest, and joy for these children." The looks on the faces of these boys from the Zapata Home attest to the fact that they are receiving that kind of love.

One of my favorite photos of my
husband taken in the mid 1970s.

Myself in 1978.

The Roloff boys as children.
L to R: Melvin, Lester, Edell.

Our precious daughters with
Lester and myself at the time
he first entered evangelism.

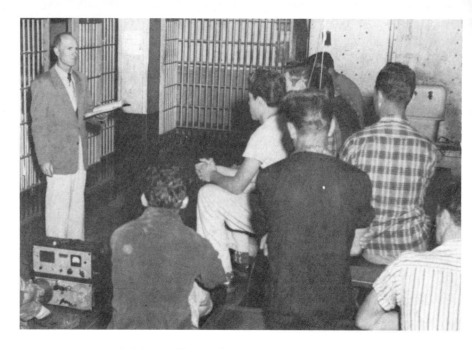

Lester at an early jail preaching service.

Rebekah girls at The People's Church in Corpus Christi. Care and prayer launched this rescue work for girls in need of help and hope.

We could not know the first time Lester went to jail on February 12, 1974, that he would be back in jail on June 21, 1976, for five days and face a continuing battle with the state of Texas Welfare Department. Of this experience my husband has staunchly declared: "I plan to fight on to the highest court in the land for our God-given protection under the Constitution and also the wonderful Word of God."

The girls who come to Rebekah Home will leave with sewing and other skills—the result of patient and loving help from those who are interested in them and their future welfare.

Girls from the Bethesda Home.
They came to us disillusioned, bewildered, embittered, and sad. They will leave transformed—reborn, self-confident, and able to take their place in society.

time. The house was 150 years old when I first saw it, and there was a log cabin about 155 years old.

We walked all over the 273 acres and through and around that magnificent old house, but I had no leading or impression that it should be ours. As I looked at the original log cabin and then gazed up into the most majestic trees I'd ever seen and out across the private twenty-acre lake filled with fish, I said to Al, "For $185,000 it's beyond our reach. All I need is a place for alcoholics."

My wife, Marie, Mrs. Gene Price, and Mrs. Earl Goodman went by car to see the place later. Marie came back and couldn't get over its beauty. "All those pine trees, and that lake, and that house . . . oh, Lester, it's delightful from every viewpoint!" She was effusive in her appreciation of all it had to offer. What woman wouldn't be!

Six months later I found I was thinking about the place—it was located in Culloden, Georgia, near Atlanta, where we have more friends than in any other place (a city at that time of nearly two million). The greatest interest in our ministry on the part of people and preachers was coming from this area of the country. I reminded myself of its privacy—four miles to the closest neighbor and with no road running by it. It had two runways which would make it convenient and timesaving for us to go and come. I heard that still, small, inner voice reminding me that I was traveling east of the Mississippi as much as west of the Mississippi in meetings in Florida, Georgia, Virginia, Tennessee, Alabama, and the Carolinas. The voice said it's only a half day's flight from Corpus Christi to Culloden. I had been told that fifty head of beautiful white-faced cattle would go with the selling price. I could see the heavy grass that would furnish nearly year-round pasture.

I visualize it as a place, not just for the down-and-outs, but for the up-and-outs. It would furnish a tremendous setting for our Bible conferences. Friends of the ministry could go there and see one of the most historic and beautiful places a person could ever set eyes on.

I went through a lot of anguish over the place, and finally I said, "Lord, I just can't take on any more debt." And He said, "You aren't going to have to go into debt; it will be paid for in cash, $108,000." That was a lot less than the selling price. I wondered if I was really hearing correctly; this was $32,000 less than the first price offered.

I went to Atlanta to the bank and talked with three bankers—Mr. Peacock, Mr. Duncan, and Mr. Trailor. I ended up putting five thousand dollars down on the property. Brother Jerry Falwell and one of his good men, Brother Smith—and also Brother Bob Barber—came down to meet us there and were amazed at the beauty and the wonderful location and the possibilities of a work there.

On November 6, 1965, we had nine hours of radio time generously donated by Mr. Rumminger and WAVO, and we had access to three telephones. We also had an open house in the lovely old antebellum home on the property. We were to see the greatest demonstration of giving that we had ever seen in the history of the Enterprises, but not before the Lord tried our faith to the utmost. After all of those plans—the radio time, the open house—I felt a compulsion to withdraw our offer. I went to the same three bankers the next day, on a Monday, and told them I felt we should back out.

One of the bankers said, "You don't think you'll get

your five thousand dollars back, do you?" I answered him, "No, sir." I guess I was a little bold, for I said, "If you were to give us the place and the Lord didn't want us to have it, it would cost too much. And at this point, I'm not quite sure He wants us to have it so we'll just not worry about that money."

That night the Lord entered the cemetery of my buried dreams and told Lazarus to come forth. You see, everything I ever want to do has to die before it can get resurrected. It was only after I had given it up that God gave the assurance He did want us to have it and that it was to be our permanent City of Refuge. Since then, through all these years, I've had perfect peace about the move to Culloden.

On a Sunday night in 1965 we lacked $38,000. The next morning we lacked $10,000. And, strangely, I felt the Lord didn't want me to ask for money or pledges. The total amount was not due until July 16, and this was July 4.

God had told me initially that it would all be paid for. It was a great exercise of soul faith, with tears and testings.

We were holding a camp meeting—precious "pilgrims," friends of the Enterprises, with trailers and campers and tents had made their way to the property to join us in praying and singing and to testify that they still believed that "Christ is *the* Answer." I had gone to the banker and asked, "Will you let me burn the note at our noon meeting?" He had said, "Yes," and brought it out.

That noon, moments before I was going to burn the note, a man in the crowd walked up to me, handed me a signed blank check and said, "This is for whatever you still lack." And so we were debt free!

I'll never forget what that man and his wife said as they handed me that blank check. "We believe this place must be *debt free to set men free.*"

And so with great rejoicing we claimed again the Scriptures, "Now the just shall live by faith," and "Without faith it is impossible to please God."

There were alcoholics and other sinners saved at the meeting that night! What a testimony to God's faithfulness and the love and caring of His people!

Alfred Edge, vice-president of Roloff Evangelistic Enterprises, has been a director on the board since its inception. On the occasion of my husband's birthday a few years ago Alfred said what many have often expressed: "I am sure no other human could possibly know the burdens, problems, and also the joys in these many years. The accomplishments from the first annual directors' meeting to the last directors' meeting are almost unbelievable. It is not the directors who are responsible for the day-in and day-out operation of the Roloff Evangelistic Enterprises. Rather, our duties are to review all of the activities, plus counsel with Brother Roloff from time to time. My association with the Enterprises is an honor and a privilege; and if all who read this knew what I knew, they would agree with me."

"The song I associate with Brother Roloff and the Enterprises is 'Others.' His entire ministry is unselfishly dedicated to *others.*"

Lord, help me live from day to day
In such a self-forgetful way
That even when I kneel to pray
My prayer shall be for others.

Others, Lord, yes, others,
Let this my motto be,
Help me to live for others,
That I may live like Thee.[4]

---

[4]Charles D. Meigs, "Others." Copyright 1956 by Singspiration. All rights reserved. Used by permission.

31

Wrecks Rebuilt

As our ministry became more widely known, it became the dumping ground for the unwanted and the unlovely. Yet we saw it as our greatest challenge. We knew that wrecks could be rebuilt and vessels remade from these destitute and despairing alcoholics and narcotic addicts.

Lester told radio listeners, "My little spiritual plane is still landing on runway sixteen—Philippians 1:6: 'Being confident of this very thing, that He which hath begun a good work in you will perform it until the day of Jesus Christ.' God has started the new 'City of Refuge' project, and He will complete it and provide for our ever-growing needs."

The Lord speaks to my husband in some unusual ways. Some months before venturing forth in faith into the new City of Refuge, the Lord reminded him to ask for big things; and that just as He took the jewels away from the Egyptian women and gave them to the Israelite slave women, He would take valuable things away from the world and give them to us (as Christians) because "All things are yours." At that time my husband said, "Lord, the Enterprises' work could use a million dollars."

Lester had read a 1965 column by Ann Landers that said one thousand new alcoholics were born every day. "Surely we can win some of them to Jesus," he said to me one day. "I've been thinking for a number of weeks about the need for a revival of sacrificial giving, and I believe now is the time. But isn't it a thrill to be a partner in a ministry that's wholly of faith? For when help comes, we know it's the Lord who gives it!"

He urged friends of the ministry to "make a faith promise and then pray it down." God directed Lester's attention to Job 34:32, "That which I see not teach Thou me . . . ." He wrote in the *Faith Enterprise*:

God is permitting me to learn what I cannot see. Can't you just hear the words of Jesus as He said to Martha, "If thou wouldest believe, thou shouldest see. . . ." Believing is the first law of the spiritual life and right now I want to thank all of our precious friends for understanding as well as you have this plunge of faith. Many have been the letters which say, "We're right with you, and we admire you for your courage and faith and conviction to continue to tackle the impossible."

Out of the first eight persons who came to the new City of Refuge, four left either the same day or a few days after they came. Brother Johnnie Davis was the superintendent, and he and the other helpers, as well as my husband, found themselves begging the men, "Please stay. Don't leave; Christ is *the* Answer." My husband's understanding of these desperate men never ceases to amaze me. He told us that as he was flying along, he knew the heartache and humiliation that finally brought these alcoholics and narcotic addicts our way. They came because it would keep them out of jail or reform school, or it was a means to get out of one of those places where they were already serving time, and they came with trembling fear.

From time to time he published in our monthly paper the requirements for admittance to the "City":

1. Be sure you've reached the end of yourself and know there is no other hope except Christ.
2. Make up your mind to stay ninety days.
3. No cigarettes, dope, pills, liquor, or coffee—NO TAPERING OFF!
4. All incoming and outgoing mail will be censored, including packages.
5. Even though there is no charge made, if one has an income, it should be given to the "City" as long as he is there.
6. If one leaves before ninety days, he or his loved ones should pay expenses in order that we might help somebody else.
7. A church ought to sponsor every man's coming to the "City," pray for him daily, write to him at least every week or two, and help him when he returns home.
8. We do not have a medical staff at the "City"—fact is, we cannot even allow rubbing alcohol, shaving lotion, or hair tonic with alcoholic content. But I'll tell you what we do have—Jesus the Great Physician, the Holy Spirit, the Word of God, fine Christian workers, and the prayers of thousands of people across this country that have kept us from having even one funeral and have also given deliverance to every person who has ever stayed ninety days and cooperated.

There is not enough space in this book to relate all the stories of lives salvaged and souls saved. But there are some we should share.

For many years the work at the "City" involved helping both men and women. Dormitories were built and the doors were always open to those who needed and wanted help.

Mary Smith is typical of the women who received such

help.

I came from Ohio, and I was living in sin. I was into drugs and staying in a hippie commune. I didn't care what happened to me or where I went. One day a friend told me I could have help if I came to the "City." I came in 1971, and I thought, "Well, this is not what I want to do." But when I arrived, everyone was so helpful and kind, and I couldn't believe that people could be nice to me because I wasn't a very nice person. I didn't like myself or others.

After I was here awhile, I could see the difference that Christ made in them—giving them love for people like me. I accepted the help given, Christ became a living reality in my life, and I was totally transformed. Christ is the Answer. I thank the Lord daily that I'm now free.

Mary is studying at Tennessee Temple College even as this book is being written. Her plans are, the Lord willing, to go to Mexico as a missionary and work with children.

Mary and others like her cannot say enough about "Mom" McCoy who, with quietness, patience, and Christlike love, has lived the life of godliness before them that resulted in their being willing to turn their lives over to the Lord. "Mom" has lived at the "City" for seven years. She has had threats made on her life by deranged women coming off drugs or going through alcoholic withdrawal; she has taken many a pregnant girl to the hospital and stayed with her until the baby was born and then helped the girl to make an adjustment back into normal living. "There has been much excitement and every other emotion connected with this work," she says, including "deepest joy and deepest pain."

One of the problems "Mom" McCoy has faced often is

helping a young woman get the hatred for her mother out of her system. "They rebel and do wrong and like to blame it on their mothers and, in some instances, on their fathers. They feel this gives them some kind of license for what they've been through. "Mom" says:

> I have to make them realize they are adults who have not done right and God holds each one of us accountable for our own waywardness and sinfulness. Sometimes it is a long, hard battle, but if they accept Christ—and most of them leave having made that decision—then I tell them they cannot harbor hatred for their parents and be forgiven by God. To work with them through this is to see them emerge cleansed.
>
> Many of the girls who have come to the "City" were from a fundamentalist or another kind of church background. The family may have routinely gone to church and were "religious" but not Christian. It takes some doing to make an individual realize the difference between attending church and living for the Lord.

The untiring efforts of people like "Mom" McCoy, Johnnie Davis, and others are what made the difference between success and failure of the "City." Johnnie describes the years as a time of "tears, heartaches, disappointments, and many victories." At the end of the first seven years at the new "City," Johnnie could report that more than two thousand men and women had knocked on the door at the "City" asking to come in, and most of them had left with victory in their hearts. Some leave without Christ, without hope, and unwilling to surrender all. But Johnnie says:

> The man or woman who comes and stays ninety days

never gets over what he or she learns here. It gives them something they will always cherish and treasure. They get something that will stay with them no matter where they go or what they do because it is real. We know how to help people here at the City of Refuge because we know that it is the acceptance of Jesus Christ as personal Savior that brings victory.

32

"Have Mercy . . . My Daughter Is in Trouble"

In September, 1967, in one of Lester's gospel meetings in the Fort Worth area, a desperate little girl came to him. She was in serious trouble and needed a place to go. He had no place to send her—up until that time the ministry had mainly centered on rescuing the men and boys—but he announced in the service that if any couple present would be willing to take a girl in trouble into their home, he would like to see them after the service.

Raymond and Ernestine Weatherford, who had just recently met my husband, were in the audience. After the service they asked Lester if he had found a place for the girl to go, and he replied, "Well, I've had several offers, but I was waiting for you!"

They took her into their home in Athens, Texas. Within a few weeks my husband called them again, saying he had another girl who needed a place to go. Five months later they had eight girls in their home, and the need for a permanent home for girls adrift in sin made itself felt.

The Weatherfords felt God was calling them into this work. As a result the Rebekah Home was started with one old store building that had been given to us and moved to a lot in Flower Bluff, a suburb of Corpus Christi. Two apartments and two bathrooms were put in and the Weatherfords and the girls moved in.

Those were glorious days and soon there was a need for additional living quarters for the girls who were being sent to us. House trailers were put into use, and finally the move to our present Rebekah Home site was effected.

That move came about when Mr. Alfred Edge took my husband to the property one mile outside of the city limits. Lester looked at the seventy-nine acres and said, "This is it." It was very plain to him that this was where God wanted him to build Rebekah Home.

When asked how he was going to pay for it, Lester responded, "By cash." The realtor said, "When?" and without hesitation my husband answered, "September." He put up five thousand dollars earnest money. The realtor gave him another five thousand that brought the remaining amount due down to $87,000.

Once again over the airwaves the need for launching into this work was presented. "Oh, my precious friends, as long as there is ripe grain, we dare not come out of the harvest field," Lester said with deep emotion.

All you've got to do to get interested and burdened is just to look through your own eyes at a precious girl and say, "There goes my drifting daughter," and cry like the Canaanite woman, ". . . Have mercy on me, O Lord, . . . my daughter is grievously vexed with a devil" (Matt. 15:22). And hear that blessed answer from the lips of Jesus, ". . . O woman, great is thy faith: be it unto thee even as thou wilt . . ." (Matt. 15:28). And her daughter was made whole from that very hour.

And there is not a drifting, wayward daughter anywhere who we could not make whole through the finished work of Christ on the Cross. Just as Jesus raised the dead daughter of Jairus, even so He could raise the dead daughters of sin today because He loves and cares. You and I must not do less. It's amazing what care and prayer can do.

And so care and prayer launched the rescue work for girls in need of help and hope. One week before the due date we had the total amount needed. The house trailers were moved to the property. We were soon informed by the state that we could not operate out of trailers and so work on a dormitory was begun.

We had a big old barn that we quickly converted into a "heavenly hayloft" for meetings. Carpet was laid, air conditioning put in, and it was beautified. Some of the most glorious days and weeks of our lives occurred when that loft was filled with the girls and others, and downstairs the cows mooed and the goats bleated while we held meetings.

As we began working with these girls, we realized that many of them were unwanted and consequently unloved. Lester said, "No wonder children have become embittered and even criminals at an early age. They've never seen love in those who gave them birth. The right kind of love would lock and stop the wheels of divorce, delinquency, murder, and war and turn this hell on earth into a haven of peace, rest, and joy for these children."

To the radio listeners he spoke on this need for love in a message entitled "The Greatest of These . . ." He requested they read Matthew 22:37-40; John 14:15,23; John 15:12,17; 1 John 3:14; 1 John 4:7,8; and 1 Corinthians 13. "This is the cure-all for the world, and yet the world knows very little about it," he maintained.

Love is the difference between religion and Christianity, between sincerity and the synthetic and superficial. It's the only motive for acceptable service to the Lord. "If ye love me, keep my commandments."

"A new commandment I give unto you, that ye love one another; as I have loved you."

It's the Christian's identification badge. "By this shall all men know that ye are my disciples, if ye have love one to another."

There's no way for us to keep on keeping on or to minister to the poor pieces of wrecked humanity that come to us as delinquents, narcotic addicts, alcoholics (both men and women), poor little girls in trouble—apart from the love that Jesus gives.

We've received far more condemnation and criticism than we have commendation. Our failures have been far more vicious to us than the successes and victories have been helpful, and we have to keep looking beyond the trickle of time before we can see the real reward. And yet we dare not quit or let bitterness enter, but lift our face toward Calvary and in love pray for them.

Even then we were beginning to feel the flak from those who questioned our motives, our finances, and the reasoning behind all our efforts. To such as these my husband has often replied, "Oh, how these precious rebels need our love and our help until they surrender to Christ!" But through the years we did find those such as the three juvenile and parole officers who wrote:

Thank you for the fine young man recently sent back to me. I knew he would benefit and mature greatly while with you, but in all truthfulness I must say he greatly exceeded all my expectations. I wish all the boys who come my way could spend six months with you. . . .

175

I observed the good that had been accomplished with Butch as I took him home. He was quoting Bible verses—and I know my Bible—and he was quoting accurately. . . .

I cannot tell you how much I appreciate the help you have recently given four boys from my county. Maybe someday the people from this county will realize what you are doing. . . .

The needs of both the young boys and the young girls who came to my husband's attention pressed deeply upon his mind. "There's nothing sadder than to see a generation of girls insulted and dragged into shame," he reported to readers of the *Faith Enterprise*. Readers did not know about the agonizing hours he spent in prayer asking the Lord for direction, nor could they know of the phone calls that came at all hours of the day and night. The callers would plead, "We must have help for our daughter, and we must have it *now!*" His response would be, "Bring her to us. Jesus finished all the work that ever needed to be done for boys and girls."

Early one morning in 1967 the Lord gave my husband assurance that our Christian friends and converts would be our advertising agency from that point on. The Lord also assured him they would become our bankers. "That which lives by faith and depends on Me cannot go down to Egypt for help," God was saying to my husband in the inner recesses of his soul. Lester knew "the spiritual man must walk without the aid of flesh-made crutches."

At six o'clock the phone rang and a lady from Alice, Texas, was on the other end. "Brother Roloff, do you have a need for eight thousand dollars? I would like you to have it to use until I need it."

My husband recognized God's hand and told me, "Amen, Marie! That lady is our first banker. Now we can begin our 'IS Fund.' " This meant "Interest Saving" where friends of the ministry would let us use their money, and we would send it back within three days when they needed it again. Lending money this way has been a blessed experience for those who have helped through the years. This is money they have saved and put aside for a funeral or sickness or an unexpected emergency. They could not afford to give it, but they have let us use it. To date, over a million dollars has been put to work in this manner.

That morning in 1967 Lester got up off his knees with a fresh vision of what God would have him do and reported:

This morning, as I prayed, the Lord gave me a fresh vision in connection with the story of Mephibosheth, the son of Jonathan whom David loved so dearly. Many years after Jonathan had been killed, David was the king, and he longed to do something for Jonathan's family. He sent his servant, Ziba, down to Lodebar, a place of destitution, and found Jonathan's crippled son named Mephibosheth, brought him to the king's palace, and let him put his crippled feet under the table of plenty, and cared for him the rest of his life.

As I prayed, I saw a million little Mephibosheth girls living in the land of Lodebar, in juvenile shelters, jail houses, broken homes, hippie hives, and dope dives. I saw these girls sleeping in parks and walking through the wilderness of sin. I prayed again for a thousand Zibas to give a thousand dollars each so we could go to Lodebar and bring them to the Rebekah Home and to Christ. I've been convinced a thousand times and more that Christ is

177

the Answer and He is the only Answer.

In the last week, I've seen a dozen girls already come in. . . . We've received a convict who spent fourteen-and-a-half years in the penitentiary on a life sentence. We've seen dope addicts, dope pushers, and dope peddlers saved. We've seen God perform miracles in the courtroom to keep some of our boys out of the penitentiary, and others will be facing trial in just a few days.

I saw an ungodly liquor sign which said, "If you can find a better bourbon, buy it." But I have a better statement to make—if you can find a better place to invest your money than in these precious boys, girls, men, and women who are destitute and desperate and ready to come out of Lodebar, then put it there.

After preaching for forty years, Lester could report that he had been in more than three thousand churches. In the early 1970's we saw more preachers and more churches responding to help us run to the rescue. This was a great encouragement to him. He regarded it as the Lord's fulfillment of the early morning prayer assurance in 1967.

One morning in 1972 he shared the vision and the plans that God had put upon his heart.

We've already put lumber on the new site to build a double-decker dormitory (to house about 160 new girls), a school building, and a gymnasium. And then we'll have to have a church building to seat all the people. These are emergency buildings that must be built quickly.

God has given us definite plans for a million-dollar expansion program and I'm asking our friends, churches, and various groups to join Mrs. Roloff and me in each giving one thousand dollars. God never gives me faith and conviction to ask Him for anything without giving me assurance to believe that it will be done. This ministry is now nationwide. The last four girls who have just arrived have come from Texas, Kansas, Virginia, and North Carolina. A lifelong friend who has loved us and supported us came with his little daughter this week saying, "I never dreamed, Brother Lester, that I'd have to have your help."

It's my prediction that everyone who reads this either has a son, a daughter, a mother, a dad, a loved one, or a friend who desperately needs the services of one of our homes. So think it not strange or selfish or mercenary of me to expect you to hold the rope if I'm to go down in the well. And I'm certainly human enough, and sometimes weary enough, to cry for Aarons and Hurs to hold up these hands that offer hope to the hopeless and help to the helpless, reminding you that these ministries will come to a screeching halt at the soon sound of the trumpet and the shout of our returning King.

He told us to go only till He comes, and praise God, I'd like to be coming out of Lodebar with a big load of Mephibosheths when the good news is sounded out, "The Bridegroom cometh, go ye out to meet Him!" I want the clouds to be filled with precious souls over every home that God has given us when He comes. I want the devil and his crowd to find every room and bed and chair empty one second after the shout.

33

More Ventures of Faith

For many years Lester carried within him a concern for our older Christian friends and those who had reached retirement age. Many had been a part of his ministry from his earliest days on radio. He felt a responsibility for them as they faced the sunset years of their lives. So it was that in 1969 the Peaceful Valley Home, located near Mission, Texas, in the Rio Grande Valley (approximately 150 miles south of Corpus Christi), became another venture of faith.

Those who were interested in coming to the Valley and making an investment in such a home for the rest of their lives were invited to do so. The area is surrounded by orange, grapefruit, and tangerine groves, beautiful tropical foliage, and flowers. There is an abundance of fresh fruit, vegetables, shade trees, and Christian fellowship. Much of the year this valley is bathed in sunshine. While our other homes are dedicated to rescuing the perishing, this home has become a haven where the rescuers can rest, pray, and sing together. It has become the house of prayer.

My husband once said, "We promise to care for those of you who come as if you were our own mother or dad, and we will be as kind to you as grace can make us." That has never been difficult, and it has always lived up to its name: the Peaceful Valley Home.

About this same time Lester was flying through a storm and found himself out over the Gulf of Mexico for more than four hours. He landed in Crestview, Florida, with minimum fuel and a tremendous load—five girls, four of whom were pregnant. One girl had her baby shortly after they landed, and for the first time in his then five or six thousand hours of flying, he was convinced it would be right to ask the Lord and God's people to rally for a twin-engine plane. It would save many hours of his flying time and would add greatly to the safety of those on board. It wasn't long thereafter that the provisions were met and the Enterprises was able to procure the kind of plane he needed. Once again God had proven Himself faithful through His people who cared.

The number of girls in the Rebekah Home was now growing so quickly that they were able to join my husband in various cities on gospel tours. They gave their testimonies and sang. What a blessing this proved to be! And so another need presented itself—a bus was needed to transport them in safety and comfort from one place to another. Here also the need was presented, and before we knew it, the bus was a part of the ministry!

Reporting on all that was happening and the ever-present needs, Lester wrote:

When I land tonight or tomorrow, the plane will be filled with boys and girls who either must go to the prison of punishment or to one of our places of love and hope. If God brought a Daniel through the lions' den unscratched, the Hebrew children through the fire without being burned, the pastor at Jerusalem out of jail through the prayers of the church—and would shake a jail to pieces to get two of His beaten and bloody preachers out—if our kind heavenly Father notes the sparrow's fall, surely He cares when a young girl or boy falls.

But remember, God's plan was a *man* and His program

is a *person,* and you could be the person. I'm not asking you to do what you can, but I'm asking you to do what you can't!

Such was his way of challenging people to launch out in faith. He also said,

I promise you that once you step through the gates of pearl and walk one block down the streets of gold, you'll enter heaven's concert hall and praise God for the privilege of sharing with others.

Why, I'd feel like a backslider if I begged a banker to loan us what God's people ought to have the privilege of giving. When God told me our friends and His friends would be our bankers, a new day dawned. Since that day, the clouds have rifted and the burdens lifted. The Midianites have invaded our land, but give us six thousand Gideons, who will break their pitchers, expose their lamps, and blow their trumpets at the same time, and we'll finish a big job and start another one.

Only God could inspire him with new thoughts and fresh ways of phrasing things as they continued to pour forth in a seemingly never-ending stream of motivating words:

Let's have five faithful days of fervent praying and fasting that God will once more make bare His mighty arm to defeat the foe, maintain the flow, help us to sow, and we'll continue to go until many others shall glow with the warmth of the gospel of Jesus Christ.

We had an office now in Newton, Kansas, and another home for boys at Zapata, Texas (ninety miles southwest of

Corpus Christi). The property for the home in Zapata formerly had been a government radar tracking-station. It consisted of three two-story barracks, a cafeteria, a gymnasium, and an administration building. It had been closed by the government and sold to a private individual who donated it to the Roloff Evangelistic Enterprises in 1972 for the purpose of using it as a home for delinquent boys.

A work for boys had been started in Katy, Texas, and in Fredericksburg, Oklahoma, in the intervening years. But the need for something larger and more stable had shown itself many times. Since the beginning of the Anchor Home for Boys under the supervision of Mr. and Mrs. Harmon Oxford, hundreds of boys in trouble have come each year, many from jails and detention homes, and most of them have been saved and have found a new direction for their lives. My husband could say in June, 1976: "Our boys and girls are making good Christians and Americans. There are no flag-burners in our homes. We are for *God* and *country!*"

34

The Years Bring Changes

The last of the 1950's brought a wedding to our family. Our daughter Elizabeth married Clinton Twaddell while they were both students at Baylor in 1957. Daughter Pam married David Wright in 1961. After our grandchildren started arriving, another dimension was added to our lives, as any grandparent knows.

In February, 1962, Mother Roloff went to be with the Lord. Of his mother's death Lester said at her funeral that Proverbs 31 fitted her well. Hebrews 11:4 also could be applied to her life—she "being dead yet speaketh."

In 1966 my beloved mother passed on to her eternal reward, and "Papa" Roloff died in 1967. Then in 1968 God took to Himself the last of our parents when my father died.

The 1970's were to bring great triumphs to the work of Roloff Evangelistic Enterprises, as well as great heartaches. It began in September, 1970, when the Gulf Coast was hit with the most dangerous and destructive storm any of us had ever experienced. "Celia," as the storm was called, completely lost her temper and got out of control as she focused her eye on the "Sparkling City by the Sea," our own Corpus Christi.

My husband said of it that it was God making bare His majestic arm of power to leave anybody alive after such a storm—a great miracle of deliverance. The winds got as high as 180 miles an hour and came lashing and crashing, snapping telephone and power poles as if they were toothpicks.

We saw radio and television towers fall across streets. Big trucks were lifted off of the ground. Cars were stacked on top of each other. Steel beams in airplane hangars were twisted like baling wire. Possessions bought with a lifetime of savings were blown away in an instant. Trees that had taken a generation to grow were stacked along the curbs. Business buildings were destroyed. Large private homes were unroofed and in many instances the walls fell.

But what of our home? And what of the Lighthouse? And what about the valley with all of its lovely fruit and the buildings? *Untouched!* We did lose electric power and with it refrigeration and the deep freeze units. But not a drop of water nor a broken windowpane was to be found in our little frame house and one-car garage.

At the Rebekah Home "Celia" blew some shingles off of the roof and dumped water on the carpets. And some of the house trailers were damaged beyond repair. But even though "Celia" came as a curse, she left as a blessing. God protected his children, and nine girls accepted the Lord at the Rebekah Home during the height of that storm.

Friends from across the country finally got through to us and wanted to know the extent of the damage and what they could do. Actually that storm hastened the building of more badly needed dormitories and facilities at the Rebekah Home.

The prophet long ago said, ". . . the Lord hath his way in the whirlwind and in the storm . . ." (Nah. 1:3). We were able to tell everyone that Romans 8:28 is still in force!

The storm became the basis for some spiritual analogies that worked their way into Lester's messages. He reminded us that storms just about always lie across the path of progress; but the flame and flood and storm have never stopped the saints who look for the lesson and pinpoint the purpose of such an experience.

One of the first things my husband and I did after the storm was to work our way through blocked, debris-filled streets to the airport. We saw the destroyed hangar and a plane lying on its back on top of another plane—and it was the same color and make as ours. Our hearts sank, but we walked a little further and there we saw our beautiful and useful Aztec. We both ran, and we hugged an engine, and in tears we thanked the Lord for protecting such a valuable and expensive piece of equipment. My husband looked at me and said, "Marie, praise God! Psalm 121 still works!"

One of the hardest things we have had to do is to turn boys and girls away. "No room in the inn" is literally what we have had to say on many occasions. In the fall of 1971 we found our homes filled to capacity. Jeremiah the prophet said, "The harvest is past, the summer is ended, and we are not saved" (Jer. 8:20). Lester quoted the writer of Proverbs: ". . . he that sleepeth in harvest is a son that causeth shame" (Prov. 10:5). And he reminded our supporters about what Jesus said in Matthew's Gospel: ". . . The harvest truly is plenteous, but the labourers are few" (9:37).

Fall was always a happy time around our farm, even though it was a hard time because there was so much work to be done. It was a hasty time and it was a helping time. It was an honorable time and it was a housing time for us to put the grain and the cotton into a safe place. But you know, the harvest doesn't wait. We either reap it or it ruins and rots.

The farmer would become desperate if he had no barn in which to place the grain after it was harvested.

186

We all knew Lester was referring to the needs for the homes. Much had been accomplished, however, in that year since "Celia" came through Corpus Christi.

In Hattiesburg, Mississippi, Brother Charles Williams and the Central Baptist Church made it possible for us to acquire 210 acres of land on Blue Lake. It was a beautiful setting that had formerly been used for drinking parties. Ground was broken, and a large dormitory was built. It came to be called the Bethesda Home. Brother Harmon Oxford and his wife moved from Frederick, Oklahoma, where we had a work for boys. At first the home was used to house these boys in trouble. Later Mr. and Mrs. Hubert Barnwell came to help manage the home, and it became a haven for unwed pregnant girls and other girls who were in trouble. *Bethesda* means *House of Mercy*, and this home has always lived up to its name.

The construction, growing, and expansion continued in every area of the Enterprises' work. It was enough to make my head swim at times. Our longest arm and loudest voice, however, continued to be the radio ministry.

In May, 1972, Lester and I moved into a lovely, large new home on the acreage where the Rebekah Home and other buildings were already located. Brother Johnnie Davis and his helpers built the house with gifts sent for that purpose by our many friends across the nation.

Another 118 acres of land next to our Corpus Christi property was purchased. It had a runway on it for our plane, and we could farm some of the remaining acres. During the summer of 1972, workers built another big two-story building; it became the Rebekah Christian School. Here the girls, in addition to their academic subjects, are taught the Bible, sewing, nutrition, and how to be ladies and home-makers.

This land became ours in an unusual way. My husband often used to stand looking at this acreage, praying that it could become a part of the Enterprises' plan. The week before we planned to buy it, a wealthy man purchased it instead. But just before it came time to sign the papers, the man was killed. We were offered the property and, of course, could not say "no." Lester preached a sermon on miracles and why he believes in them.

It's scriptural and normal—starting with the new birth which brings a new life.

It's just putting to work the gift of faith which God has measured to every man who asks.

It glorifies and pleases God.

A miracle is a human impossibility. It's an event beyond the power of any known physical law to produce. It's a supernatural occurrence produced only by the power of God, and Nicodemus was right when he came to Jesus by night and said, "No man doeth miracles except God be with him."

We're either lost, or spiritually retarded and invalids, if God is not performing miracles through us. If man can take raw material and put it together and make an airplane which is called a flying miracle; if man can take a wrecked car and rebuild it and make it like new; if man can take a bunch of dirty rags and make white, clean writing paper on which love letters and good news can be sent; then why would you think it strange that God, who made the universe, the world, and all that therein is, could take a human instrument and work miracles with him?

You, like Nicodemus, could raise the question, "How can these things be?" The Holy Spirit can empower a soul to become the tool in God's hand to hit a supernatural lick. . . .

Since Christ is real and the Bible exists, miracles are a must if we follow Him.

Faith pays no attention to form, custom, or tradition and plows right through opposition and misunderstanding. But faith can never obtain the approval or the license or acceptance from the world. It will be branded a renegade or rebel—noncooperative and hard to get along with. Faith leads a lonely and isolated life, and its one distinct joy and reward is that it pleases God.

A miraculous ministry lives in and on the Word of God and prayer. We prayed for laborers, and the Lord thrust them on the field. We prayed for provisions to build dormitories and buildings to provide homes for two hundred girls, for alcoholics, narcotic addicts, and rebels, and God provided. We prayed for such as these to be saved, and God saved them. We prayed for the boys and for a chapel down the Intracoastal Canal, and God moved. We prayed and then plunged as we believed for two million dollars worth of expansion—and now we've already passed the halfway mark for this year.

When the world questions, "Where are the miracles?" we can answer, "Here they are."

At the close of 1972, we could say it was the greatest year the ministry had ever known. The last of December that year saw four days of dedication. We dedicated the chapel at the Intracoastal Canal; our home; the land adjoining the Enterprises' property; a big new boys' home at Zapata, Texas; five new units at the Peaceful Valley Home; the big two-story dormitory at the Rebekah Home; the two-story Rebekah School; and the People's Church, which is nearly two blocks long.

35

"If It Wasn't for the Lighthouse . . ."

One of the favorite songs of the Rebekah girls and my husband is "If It Wasn't for the Lighthouse, Where Would This Ship Be?"

The Lighthouse work in some ways was a stepchild of the Enterprises. Because of its location, forty miles from civilization, it had no running water and only had simple buildings, arrangements, and facilities. The day finally came when we were able to put a diesel engine down there to provide lights, refrigeration, and a deep freeze. For many years all the drinking water had to be hauled in, and there was no place for showers. In spite of such inconveniences, however, it was a healthy place with lots of fresh air, fresh fish, fruit from the valley, vegetables from the gardens, and love. The latter, of course, was the most important ingredient.

It was a happy day when a chapel was built for the boys, but within months, it was needed to house beds and boys. A plea finally went out—we had to build a decent dormitory. Lester said at the time:

> Nearly every boy we have now, or have ever had, would be in prison but for the Lighthouse. And I would say without doubt that many who have come to the Lighthouse through the years would be dead by now had

it not been for the light from this old Lighthouse that sits on the spoil bank.

The large dormitory for the boys was completed in 1972. What rejoicing there was down on the Intracoastal Canal! The Lighthouse is the second-oldest home we have and, in actuality, the "home" the boys had all those years left much to be desired in the way of comfort. But there wasn't a boy who came there who didn't prefer it to being behind bars in a jail or living in a reform school.

I think, for instance, of the four boys from Milledgeville, Georgia, who each had been sentenced to six years in prison. After two of our converts gave their testimonies, the judge changed his mind and offered the four boys the alternative of coming to the Lighthouse. Within weeks each boy was transformed and born again. After they were with us one year, my husband was able to recommend to the judge that they be allowed to return to society. They went back "another way" to take their places in the world as responsible human beings. Time after time—we long ago lost count—we have seen this happen. In one recent year fifteen boys surrendered their lives to the Lord and went off to Christian schools and colleges to prepare for a life of special service.

Many of our Lighthouse boys have ended up marrying our Rebekah Home girls, and these have turned out to be some of the most beautiful married couples you could find on the face of the earth today. I think of Ronnie and Reneé Doring and Kim and Barbara Bower. Each of these and other couples have said, in their own ways, that their salvation and spiritual growth they owe to Christ first, and then to the work of our Enterprises' staff and my husband. "If it wasn't for the Lighthouse, where would this ship be?"

is a comment we have heard in many versions hundreds of times.

Lester has often said, "We work with tomorrow's criminals today, but by God's grace we have been faithful and worked with these boys and girls, and we have seen victory in the lives of thousands of them, even rapists and murderers. We know that Christ is the Answer." But you can be certain that when you are on the firing line for God, the devil will be working overtime to thwart the work.

And then it happened!

On July 25, 1975, at 5:35 p.m., Stan Williams, superintendent of the Lighthouse, knocked at our door. "Brother Roloff, I've got bad news for you. The Lighthouse dormitory just burned to the ground!" Along with two newsmen from the Corpus Christi *Caller-Times*, Lester flew there immediately and knelt at the edge of the ashes with the boys. One boy held the American flag above his head, and they all began to sing, "Had it not been for the light from the Lighthouse, where would we boys be?"

We praised God that fifty of the boys were in chapel and others were in town helping Brother Stan when this had happened. Clothes, suitcases, new double bunk beds (with drawers in them that had just been built), a big kitchen, a dining room (with all the tables and chairs), and the grocery room (it had just been restocked)—all of it was gone.

Even at this tragic time, the Lord impressed upon Lester's heart the need to speak to the brokenhearted boys.

Isaiah 61:1-4: "The Spirit of the Lord God is upon me; because the Lord hath anointed me to preach good tidings unto the meek; he hath sent me to bind up the brokenhearted, to proclaim liberty to the captives, and the opening of the prison to them that are bound; To proclaim the acceptable year of the Lord, and the day of vengeance of our God; to comfort all that mourn; To appoint unto them that mourn in Zion, to give unto them *beauty for ashes*, the oil of joy for mourning, the garment of praise for the spirit of heaviness; that they might be called trees of righteousness, the planting of the Lord, that He might be glorified. And they shall build the old wastes, they shall raise up the former desolations . . ." (italics added).

Boys, we are going to glorify God in this fire. Job once was in the ash pile, and God gave Job twice as much as he once had. We are going to claim, by faith, twice as many of you boys as we've ever had, and twice as big a building to put you all in.

Only the house has burned, lads, not the Light. The Light from the Lighthouse is fireproof. I know that every earthly possession of the Lighthouse and of you boys is in these ashes, but let us claim Isaiah 61:3, that God will "give unto us beauty for ashes."

A few days later we had a glorious experience. After the fire my husband had immediately called the Austin Land Commission to ask about prospects for rebuilding the dormitory. He was offered no encouragement. Our hearts were deeply troubled and saddened. For well over twenty years the Light from our unusual Lighthouse had pointed hundreds of wayward boys to the Father's house. Everyone else along the Intracoastal Canal was receiving permits for building, but now we were being told that our request would not be considered. My husband reminded the Austin Land Commission that our Lighthouse had often served as a sort of clearinghouse and had long been the helping hand for fishermen and others in trouble because of our radio and our plane. After he had received no encouragement, Lester got in his plane and flew to the Lighthouse to join the boys in the chapel. His heart was heavy. That particular morning, instead of talking and giving the boys a message, Lester asked them to share.

A tall boy stood and said, "Brother Roloff, I got saved last night, and I have a confession to make. I struck the match that burned the building and destroyed everything, and I am willing to face my punishment."

God had already begun to give us beauty for ashes. The boys gathered around and offered their forgiveness to the tall boy, and my husband came home and said, "Honey, a sweeter spirit I have never seen nor known. Glory has begun to come out of those flames. The Light is going to burn brighter. *It will never go out.*"

Later, at 5:00 one Sunday morning, my husband knelt to pray with forty girls after their all-night prayer meeting following the fire. Once again the Lord impressed upon Lester the need to speak his heart. Victory had come.

1 Thessalonians 5:18: "In every thing give thanks: for this is the will of God in Christ Jesus concerning you."

By faith we trust Thee, Lord, and rejoice in what has been done and that all of the boys out at the Lighthouse this very moment are saved. Thank You, Lord, for the stabilizing of their faith; for their tears; for the closeness of the boys to each other and to You.

And now we are looking forward to the leadership for the future—just what Thou would have us to do. Give me a message and, Lord, show us that our faith is to be fireproof and that nothing permanent has burned, but just the temporary building that we might move on to something bigger and better for Thee.

36

Cease and Desist

Every one of our buildings meets the standards and requirements set forth by the state in which it is located. All new buildings have been built according to the state's requirements, including the sprinkler systems, the arrangement of the rooms, the kitchen, and specifications for other rooms. Our buildings are among the most spotless and sanitary you could possibly find anywhere. Our people are well and healthy, as are the babies born to the girls. Yet in 1971 we were faced with shutting down our work unless we conformed to rules and regulations that would have greatly increased the cost of our operation without improving on what we were doing. We continued to believe, as Lester had once said:

When boys and girls sin, they need a Savior.
When babies are placed in a home, it ought to be a born-again, Bible-believing, praying home.

We faced our first tragic crisis on this matter when we received a letter from the Texas Welfare Department advising us to "cease and desist" because our rules did not conform to theirs.

My husband looked at me in disbelief. We had saved the state many millions of dollars during twenty years in our rescue ministries. Never had we received a penny of tax money from the government—it was God's people who had faithfully supported the work. And yet the state felt they must set the rules and regulations for our work—a work for which they paid nothing.

"Licensing these homes is as unnecessary and wrong as licensing a church," my husband contended. "At issue is the constitutional principle of separation of church and state. This plainly is government interference with religion."

People asked, "Brother Roloff, why did you react and object so strenuously? Why make such an issue out of just abiding by some rules and regulations?" My husband had answers for those questions.

Conformity brings deformity. . . . When bad men become our lawmakers, good men become our lawbreakers. I think the mother and father of Moses were lawbreakers in that they refused to give up their baby boy to be murdered by the state.

They passed a law in Daniel's day making it a violation to pray and he went to the lions' den for contempt of court. They passed another law that you had to bow to the image of Nebuchadnezzar and the three Hebrew children went to the fiery furnace for contempt of court. Vashti was put out of the palace as queen because she refused to expose her beauty at a drinking party. . . . Mordecai refused to obey wicked Haman. Jeremiah was cast into the dungeon because of his stand for righteousness. Peter went to jail because of his stand for righteousness. Paul and Silas were beaten and thrown into the jail at Philippi when revival fires began to break out in Philippi and the devil's business was injured. Joseph went to jail for refusing the overtures of a lustful woman. . . .

And without feeling sorry for myself or complaining, I face a fine and a jail sentence—and possibly a prison sentence—for doing the very thing God has told us to do and for the ministries He had unbelievably blessed.

Now in answer to the question, "Why not get a license?", my question is, "Why should we have to have a license to run a church home any more than we would have to have a license to run the church?" It actually means that we take God's money and let the state, which is altogether unprepared to run a Christian home, run the home.

There are thirty requirements in the little brown book prepared by the welfare department, most of which are unreasonable. They do not approve of our diet, even though we've had healthy girls and boys and never had a death. They do not approve of our discipline, even though it has worked. They do not approve of our staff, even though they have done a job that is unmatched and unparalleled in this nation. Our superintendents would not meet their requirements—fifteen hours of social study every two years and a college degree. And only the Lord knows the changes that would be brought about from year to year.

They are not satisfied without psychological and psychiatric help which we've never needed. The intake studies and records would take three or four secretaries. The number of workers they require is one to every eight girls, which would mean thirty-five or forty workers with three hundred girls, and there is no need to waste God's money and beds on a bunch of unnecessary workers. A long-haired, cigarette-smoking welfare worker said to one of our boys at the Anchor Home, "We'll soon fix it so that you can wear your hair as long as you want to."

The conspiracies to wreck these three homes are unbelievable. One newspaper said that we are as crooked as the stock market, that we've never given an account to anybody concerning the funds; and yet the Internal Revenue has checked us twice and given us the best report that could be given. The same newspaper said that we took a little girl out of the hospital after she had had her baby, when we were keeping pregnant girls, and that we put her to work in the field in the hot sunshine two days after the baby came.

The paper said we hired a fund raiser, which we have never done and never will. The paper accused us of selling babies, which we have never done.

The welfare department took advantage of a little girl that we took in twice. She left in bitterness, and I had said to her, "When you need help, call me." And she did. She went to Hattiesburg where we have a girls' home and had all the liberty and the freedom that any home could give. This home is run by the same standards as our Texas homes. But when she came back, the welfare department and a television station got hold of her, put this girl on television to expose her sin and shame, and got her to say that if we had taught her sex education, this probably would not have happened. They have condemned us for letting the girls get up to give their testimonies, yet they urged one to give her testimony of sin and shame.

The tactics of the welfare department cannot be our tactics. They have taken the authority away from the dad and the mother and invaded the sanctity of the home in teaching children to depend on the welfare department and the state rather than on the parents. Now they have invaded the sacredness of the church as much as to say, "You haven't got sense enough to operate your home without our help." It's a Christless program they have because they do not present Christ as the only hope for defeated children.

Jesus was crucified for the confession that He was King. We face the same issue today. I believe Jesus is King and His Word is true. I have no right to go by the welfare department's little brown book so long as I have the big black Book.

37

The State of Texas vs. Roloff Evangelistic Enterprises

A more glaring example of unwarranted government intervention in private church-related affairs would be difficult to find.

On August 3, 1973, a judgment was issued in the District Court of Nueces County (Texas) which read:

> Be it ordered, adjudged and decreed that Roloff Evangelistic Enterprises, hereinafter referred to as Defendant, is permanently enjoined from operating in the State of Texas any child-caring institution, agency or facility as defined in Article 695c, Section 8 (a) 1 (a) on and from October 1, 1973, unless properly licensed to operate such child-caring institution, agency or facility by the State Department of Public Welfare.

The ominous language of this judgment portended much more than the destruction of my husband's lifetime work. More than one Christian magazine, pastor, and concerned Christian worker saw it as a threat that could toll a funeral knell for every Christian day school, orphanage, college, retirement home, and even churches in what is supposed to be a free nation.

When the brutality accusation had first been triggered in 1971, our lawyer, along with the welfare department and the attorney general's office, rapidly put together an "agreed" judgment or injunction and asked my husband to sign it immediately. This meant we were agreeing to get a license for our homes. Signing this agreement was the only way we could keep them open; otherwise they would have been closed down immediately. Under tremendous duress Lester signed this injunction in order to buy some time, since at that time we had some two hundred girls in our care and most of them had no place to go. Later this brutality accusation was proven false.

It was agreed that we could keep sixteen- and seventeen-year-olds because they have never been considered children under the rules and regulations of the welfare department. Thirty days after we signed that "agreed" judgment, which was supposed to be permanent, the attorney general and the welfare department changed their minds. The "agreed" judgment became permanent for us but temporary for them. We were then assessed a $400 fine and $86 court costs. When we refused to pay and our lawyers asked the judge to let us go to jail in order to get the case into the Supreme Court of Texas, the court instructed the sheriff's department to collect the fine, and they decided to levy on the Lord's property. A member of the welfare department suggested filing on the plane, calling it our private plane, which it is not. It belongs to the Enterprises. This would certainly have grounded my husband. Rather than let them take the Lord's property, we paid cash. Immediately they filed against us again on the same charges.

The Texas Human Resources Committee was sent to Corpus Christi, and we appeared before them along with our workers and some of the girls to give testimony. This committee proved to be quite insensitive. One of the questions they raised was, "Do you think a man of God ought to be a lawbreaker?" This question was even asked by some who called themselves Christians; they did not fully understand why my husband had refused to be licensed by the state of Texas.

The general misconception of many people is that any statute passed by legislators constitutes the law of the land. But the U.S. Constitution is the supreme law of the land, and any valid statute must be in agreement. It is impossible for a law that violates the Constitution to be valid.

The Sixteenth American Jurisprudence, Second Section, Page 177, states: "No one is bound to obey an unconstitutional law and no courts are bound to enforce it."

The First Amendment to the Constitution guarantees complete religious liberty and separation of church and state. The Fourteenth Amendment says: "No state shall make a law that shall take away these privileges." Yet the state of Texas and the welfare department said we were breaking the law.

"If loving and living for others is a crime," my husband said, "I will have to rejoice as a criminal and be exceeding glad."

We Christians must recognize there are legitimate fields of governmental regulations. We agree with Lawyer Wyatt Libscomb on this and his stated belief in God ordained government. He intended it to reign over men within certain boundaries. But the issue we faced, as our lawyer friend pointed out, went much deeper than merely applying for a license from the state of Texas. The issue definitely is separation of church and state. If the state takes upon itself the licensing of Christian charity, then it also takes upon itself other powers that do not belong to it.

202

Christian charity has saved taxpayers millions of dollars and will continue to do so. Christian charity is not supported by the state. And it is easily demonstrated that Christian people are capable of managing and governing their own affairs. Our lawyer friend made this observation: "Because Christian charities are the actions of worship, and are therefore a part of their inalienable right to worship Almighty God, and because Christian charity is supported by the giving of Christians rather than the treasury of the state, government has neither the moral right nor the spiritual right to enforce by legal might its regulations upon Christian worship in deed. The state is wrong to require a license to worship God in deed."

My husband has repeatedly emphasized that he is not against the state nor is he against the welfare department. He states, "I believe that every state home ought to have a license. I believe that every church that takes state money ought to be under a license. But with me it is not a matter of preference, it is a matter of conviction."

38

The Attack

Faith magazine's September/October, 1973, issue, in an article written by Elmer I. Rumminger, managing editor, described what it called "The Attack" against my husband and the Enterprises' work:

From several sources, I have pieced together the story of how the present problem started. A divorced mother, who had been granted legal custody of her daughter by a court, placed her daughter in the care of the Rebekah Home for Girls. The ex-husband visited the home. He claims that he saw his daughter being mistreated. The father lodged a formal complaint against the home with the County Attorney's office. Deputy sheriffs were sent to investigate. The girl herself did not sign a complaint, but the deputies obtained the names of several other young women who constituted a rebellious clique. These girls were taken to the county attorney's office where they gave signed statements alleging various types of "mistreatment" at the home. According to his attorney, Roloff has never been given copies of all of these charges so that he can respond to each of them specifically.

The Corpus Christi *Caller-Times*, learning of the accusation printed a vitriolic denunciation of Roloff's ministries. The story is a model of slanted "reporting" and conviction by innuendo and accusation. Several of Roloff's constituency with legal backgrounds have recommended strongly that he file a libel suit. . . . I am not surprised that the *Caller-Times* would print its derogatory story without a thorough investigation of the facts or any apparent attempt to present a balanced picture. Wild accusations make good copy and increase newspaper circulation, and the average reporter salves his conscience with the sophistry that the innocent will be vindicated—eventually. Besides—a *preacher* accused of wrongdoing! That's just too juicy to pass up!

It *does* surprise me, however, that anyone would *believe* the newspaper reports of the allegations of mistreatment. I have visited the Roloff ministries on numerous occasions and talked at length with graduates of the homes, as have hundreds of pastors and evangelists and thousands of Christian laymen who have responded to Roloff's frequently broadcast "open-door" policy. In the face of the overwhelming testimony of such a broad spectrum of responsible witnesses, it is incredible that any sensible person would place a shred of credence in the accusations of a dozen teen-aged delinquents.

Newspaper reports say that there are sixteen signed statements, but a Roloff spokesman believes only a dozen girls were involved. Half of them later repented and asked forgiveness for having lied. But the damage had already been done. The inexorable wheels of government had been set in motion against the Enterprises.

The District Court of Nueces County made no express findings of any abuses or mistreatment at the homes in its August 3 judgment. The judgment instead directs its main thrust against Roloff's lack of a license for the three juvenile facilities, while hinting at the alleged abuses.

This article reported accurately that, among other things,

we would have to conform to the requirements of the state department of welfare and submit to inspections by their agents at any time.

Such inspections we did not fear; we had nothing to hide and our facilities were what the *Houston Post* described as "sparkling." This same edition of the Houston paper suggested the Texas Welfare Department might have greedy motives in wanting us uprooted and out of the way so they could take over the beautiful facilities.

What we would also have to submit to, however, was allowing state agents to interview any child or staff members in private at any time they chose. We had already seen what could happen when a few rebellious girls were singled out to be interviewed, and at any given time you will find new girls in our homes whose rebellious spirits are evident. These girls have not been with us long enough to benefit from the consistent discipline, the interaction with the other girls, and the help that inevitably takes place, resulting in dramatic transformations of their lives. Also, all records and documents of the facilities would have to be made available to welfare personnel upon request.

A full-scale war developed when newspaper, radio, and television media distorted information. Everything was slanted to destroy our image, to make us appear cruel and unloving and in need of the kind of supervision the welfare department was capable of giving. Our finances were called into question, and my husband was ridiculed and called such names as "a hell and damnation preacher," "a one stud-hoss evangelizer," "a master of the quick emotional switch," "one of the great weepers of our era," "God's freelancer," "a millionaire evangelist," and "the Texas evangelist who has more irons in more fires than Elmer Gantry or Marjoe ever dreamed of."

Lester unashamedly wept on the phone, wept before the heads of the welfare department, wept before the governor's committee, and wept and prayed in the attorney general's office. Yet there was no mercy nor consideration. There was agreement that this was a unique work, that no other home was meeting the needs we were meeting in quite the way we were meeting them, and that there was no other place quite like ours.

A great Freedom Rally was held in Austin, Texas, on October 16, 1972, the day following the judgment. A succession of young men and women testified about the changes in their lives because of my husband and the Enterprises' ministries. Tearful parents testified too. They told how their children, who had once been hooked on drugs, illicit sex, witchcraft and were into all sorts of crime and sordid living, had been saved and reclaimed to physical, spiritual, and mental health.

One of the girls told of the horrors of state mental hospitals where she had been confined until coming to us. She had been tied to her bed after repeated suicide attempts in the state-operated place. Dramatically she contrasted the repressive treatment received from so-called mental health experts with our pleasant surroundings and the loving care and concern received from our people and the other girls at the Rebekah Home. This radiant girl was not the exception; she was the rule. Where mental hospitals and psychiatrists fail miserably, the regenerative power of Jesus Christ miraculously succeeds.

State Representative Joe Salem visited the Rebekah Home and conducted a personal inspection. Later he praised our operations. "I have been in hotels all over the world, but I have never stayed in one that was any nicer than the Rebekah Home for Girls," he told newspapers. "I found the home to be very, very clean and very modern. The personnel were very cooperative."

Despite efforts by public officials and other concerned individuals, the Lighthouse work was shut down on August 3, 1973. We faced shutdown of the Rebekah and Anchor Homes if we did not comply with the judge's rulings, and in November of that year all of our dormitories were empty. To supporters of the Enterprises' work, Lester reported:

As you may know, on the other side of the highway across from our place is Memory Gardens Cemetery, and now on this side is just a garden of memories. The big sign says, "Closed by the Welfare Department."

Nearly three hundred beds are empty and nearly one hundred more at the Lighthouse and at the Anchor Home for Boys. This is the most unbelievable, un-Christian, un-American, and unfair crime that's ever been committed. The killing of twenty-seven people by the homosexual in Houston recently is nothing compared to this. My girls and boys have been scattered and shattered and some are dead already. Others are back on drugs. Even as I write this the phone has rung and a little girl called to say she is on her way back to prison, and "if they had not closed the home, Brother Roloff, I wouldn't have to go to prison."

Another mother called me and said, "My daughter is ready to be sentenced to prison, and the judge is waiting on the bench until you can tell me whether or not you can take her into the Rebekah Home." Of course, I couldn't, and to prison she went.

A quarter of a century ago, when I stepped out of denominational bondage, I thought the sun had set on my ministry, but I had my directions mixed up. It was the sun coming up out of the east on the greatest ministry God has ever given me of deliverance for the people.

When I saw three hundred preachers walk into the auditorium in Corpus Christi recently, and a thousand into the Municipal Auditorium in Austin—all ready to stand with us in this hour—saying, "Whither thou goest, we will go," brother, my heart leaped with joy, and tears streamed down my face because God is faithful. There are thousands of preachers and God's dear children like that who have not and will not bow their knee to Baal or bend to the image of Nebuchadnezzar.

What would you think about the state closing the crippled children's hospitals in all of our cities and setting them out on the curbs and sidewalks in wheelchairs and on crutches and walkers? That would not be more cruel than what has happened to us. As I said before, some of our girls who had to leave the home are dead. . . .

I seek no shortcut, and I've looked in vain for the word "compromise" in the Bible. A precious mother flew with her two boys to Austin from Detroit, Michigan, called on the phone and tearfully said, "Brother Roloff, I'd rather you burn at the stake than to bend or bow or compromise. The Christian world is watching to see if you will stand."

And by the grace of God, I'll welcome the flames and the lion's den or the jail house or the prison before I'll sell my conscience and give up my liberty that was bought by the blood of Christ and brave men on bloody battlefields. . . .

A band of precious friends came into my study the other day and asked if I would be interested in running for governor, to which I said, "I could not stand the demotion." God called me to preach, and I seek no higher calling, but I do ask for liberty to preach to three hundred girls again.

In closing, I'd like to stand once again with little David, with my slingshot of faith and some smooth stones of Bible truth, and face a mean Goliath and say with him: "Is there not a cause?" Never has my soul been so bathed with so worthy a cause. We must be true and faithful.

39

To Jail

Between November of 1973 and February of 1973, in answer to the desperate pleas of parents, we allowed girls to be sent to us for help. It grieved my husband deeply to receive these phone calls. During this time I feared for my husband's life; he lost weight, became weak, and slept very little.

Finally, on January 31, the case went to court again, and Lester was found guilty. He was fined $5,400 and sentenced to five days in the county jail on contempt of court charges. He was given the opportunity, however, to present his argument on the constitutionality of state licensing of a church-operated home before the Provisions Committee of the Texas Senate.

On February 4 more than a hundred of our loyal friends and supporters crowded into the committee hearing room. They lined the wall behind the legislators, "I've been fined $5,400 and five days in jail for doing what God told me to do," he stated. "The jail sentence is to begin on Abraham Lincoln's birthday—the man who wrote the Emancipation Proclamation, and I'm trying to write another one." What was to have been a five-minute presentation turned into a three-hour session. The senators questioned Lester on the problems and accomplishments of the Rebekah Home. As a result of that meeting, his jail term was limited to one day, February 12, pending appeal to the Texas State Supreme Court, and the fine was stayed as well, pending appeal. In

March Lester wrote in the *Faith Enterprise:*

Little did I dream thirty years ago when I went Bible in hand to the sixth floor of the Nueces County Jail and the turnkey unlocked two big steel doors and let me inside so I could preach, that thirty years later, I would go through those same doors to serve a sentence for preaching and practicing that same old Book. But on February 12, 1974, I reported to the sheriff's office to serve a jail sentence under orders to purge the home of even the sixteen- and seventeen-year-old girls.

I was taken to the booking desk where I signed my name. They searched me and then led me to the I.D. Room where they put the number 54418 around my neck and took my picture and fingerprints. Then I was taken to the mattress room where I picked up a mattress without any sheets, a tin cup, and a blanket, and the turnkey once more unlocked the big doors and assigned me to a cell with many other men.

It all started forty-one years ago when God laid His hand on my life and told me to change plows and fields. But more in particular, it began thirty years ago, when mercy through this preacher began to throw a line to perishing souls by building rescue missions, cities of refuge, and homes for boys and girls. We've enjoyed nothing but victories and a healthy growth until the state welfare department picked up our keys and locked the doors to these homes in the face of an emergency, and this in spite of the fact that we had never asked for or accepted one penny of tax money and had never made a charge for any boy or girl, man or woman, who ever came to one of our six homes. It was not because of our facilities because they've been declared to be the finest in

America. It was not because they were not loved because they certainly were, by the finest people on earth. It was not because they were abused or misused or neglected. It was all because of rules and regulations designed to cut off the access road to the River of Life.

I'm not in violation according to the Word of God.

I'm not in violation according to the Constitution of the United States.

I'm not in violation according to the Declaration of Independence. . . .

I'm not in violation according to our pilgrim forefathers.

I'm not in violation according to the wishes and desires of parents and young people across America.

I'm certainly not in violation according to the teachings and practices of the church of the Lord Jesus Christ. . . . One year ago, we had three hundred girls in the Rebekah Home, many boys at the Anchor Home, and some at the Lighthouse. Now we are allowed only six girls under eighteen. This is a demonstration of judgment without mercy. . . .

I'm not going to cast away my confidence. . . . In the meantime, we shall continue to live by faith. . . . To be photographed and fingerprinted and numbered with the transgressors means nothing in the light of the need and the worthy cause for young people today. Preachers and churches, we need to get the keys back. The state was never trained and never will be trained to run our churches and our church homes and schools. When the chains go on the pulpit, the pew will lose its liberty. And when the church loses its liberty, the nation will go into captivity and final destruction.

I can wrap myself every night, no matter how many

burdens and pressures of the day, in Old Glory and sleep with a clear conscience, knowing that I've not violated the wishes and the desires and even the blood of those who soaked that flag because of their love and loyalty for the cause of liberty and freedom. To do less will make us a generation of cowards.

I may be the first to go to jail, but I'll not be the last. My family and grandchildren have suffered humiliation and embarrassment and some shame and misunderstanding because granddaddy went to jail, but your grandchildren and mine will face far more serious persecution unless the tide is turned and the church gets back its keys.

Our risen Lord did not give the keys to the state to open and close our church homes, but He gave them to the blood-bought church and to the divinely called pastor. Some churches and denominations have been lulled and led to receive state aid, which then has a right to bring state controls; but, beloved, as long as we take no tax money, state or federal, and as long as we obey the Word of God and do a good work beyond reproach, we ought not to be harassed and destroyed by inferior rules and regulations of the welfare department.

Listen to some of the calls that have come to me in just the last few days. "Our little daughter is ten years old—we can't do anything with her. Can you possibly take her?" "My little twelve-year-old boy is lying here on the floor, passed out, because of dope. Can you take him?" "Our little girl, eleven years old, has just been buried because of an overdose of dope. It's too late for her now."

In spite of the cigarette smoke of the jail, the profanity and vulgarity, the racket of rock-and-roll, and dealing of a deck of cards, and the screaming of an old television,

214

the most peaceful time I've had in years was in the Nueces County Jail. I lay on my bunk and wept and then sat and talked to a cell mostly of young criminals and was asked by many, "Will you take me?"

One young man said, "If you still have your homes fifteen years from now, I'll come as soon as I serve my time." Another one said, "If you still have a home thirty-five years from now, I'll come when I get out of prison." One family man whose wife was expecting another child said, "Could you help me and my family?" I paid the fine for one lad, took him out of jail, and plan to work with him and others of my cellmates and inmates in the days ahead.

Thank God for the privilege of sitting where they sat. I wish every preacher could spend a day or two in jail for such a worthy cause. I cannot say like Jesus, "I was in prison and you visited me not," because I had hundreds of letters with me, and the boys gathered in my cell and sat on the floor and read the mail with me and got more excited than I.

Let me say quickly, it was not pleasant, and I would not want to spend the rest of my life in jail! I, with the other prisoners, learned to appreciate the rattle of the keys, and when the turnkey came and began to rattle those keys, every eye turned toward the doors and listened for the name of the man he'd come for.

And about midnight, after we'd been racked up and our individual cells had been closed, I heard those keys and the old doors opened and somebody said, "Brother Roloff, come and bring your things." The boys raised up from their cots, looked through the bars of the cell, and in their own friendly way said, "Good-bye, Brother Roloff; don't forget us." Others said, "God bless you."

40

Good News!

Released on a writ of habeaus corpus—an order requiring that a prisoner be brought before a court at a stated time and place to decide the legality of his detention or imprisonment—Lester was free.

On March 24, 1974, he and his attorneys appeared before the nine judges of the State Supreme Court of Texas at a hearing to determine if a discharge of the charges could be obtained. The request was made on the grounds that the original judgment was ambiguous and unclear in that it did not define what age constitutes a child or children. The former policy was that individuals up to age sixteen were considered children. Between the time we had signed the earlier "agreed" judgment and October 1, 1973, the attorney general and the welfare department changed their minds about the age (see chapter 28) and the ruling was interpreted (by the state) to mean children up to age eighteen.

My husband and his attorneys argued that reinterpretation of the "agreed" judgment had voided the terms. Questions were also raised in the minds of the judges as to what constituted a child-care home. Answers from the welfare department were unclear and even contradictory.

It was while Lester was standing on the platform at Bob Jones University on May 29, 1974, ready to receive the Founder's Award for Defending the Scriptures that the president of the school whispered in his ear, "Good news, Brother Roloff!"

When it was announced that the Supreme Court of Texas had ruled favorably for the three homes, the audience rose to its feet with a standing ovation. Glory and gratitude filled our souls. It was a victory, hard-won to be sure. It overturned the earlier ruling by Attorney General John Hill that said the word *children* meant those persons under the age of eighteen.

But the Austin decision of the Supreme Court did not end the fight. If a home such as ours was to have more than six *children* (under the age of sixteen), it must have a license from the state to operate. Our Rebekah Home, at the time it was closed, had 270 girls. At least half of them were under sixteen. Although the Texas Supreme Court ruling was a victory, it was a limited one.

Shortly after this Lester wrote "Be not Weary in Well Digging." He was alluding to Galatians 6 where we are admonished not to be weary in well doing, for in due season we shall reap if we faint not. He spoke of the people of God digging wells in the book of Genesis, and then of the Philistines coming along and filling them up with dirt. Lester saw an analogy.

That's exactly what happened to us. God gave us a vision to dig wells of hope for boys and girls, and the newspapers and magazines, with the help of the welfare department, have filled them with dirt.

"And Isaac digged again the wells of water. . . " (Gen. 26:18).

Oh, we need to dig again some wells. . . . Let us not be weary in well digging, for in due season, we shall drink pure cool water!

In June Lester was invited to speak before the Corpus

Christi Press Club. It was an unusual group and the attendance was reported as being unusually large. "You've had no mercy on what we've been doing," Lester told them. "Either you ought to help homes like ours or build one yourself. Investigation of our homes and resulting unfavorable publicity have caused donations to our Enterprises' work to be $300,000 short of what we need for operating expenses. That's damage. All I'm asking is to live by the Book and build Christian homes. This is my life. This is what you ought to be helping me do instead of helping close down homes. It takes hard work and sacrifice on the part of many people to do what we've been doing all these years, but anybody can be a part of a wrecking crew."

Shortly after that our lawyers filed libel suits against those publishers and the media who had slandered Roloff Enterprises' name and viciously attacked us. He said, "We are doing this to vindicate and exonerate our name as Christians and as servants of the Lord. We are doing it in order to get in the courts our testimony of the work our supporters have done in their investment in the lives of boys and girls. We've never had a chance in court to present the other side. We are doing it in order to put the money back into the Lord's work that we've had to spend to fight for and defend the truth and boys and girls. We believe that the court ought to provide justice for the Christian as well as for the criminal."

But Lester made one thing clear. "The Lord has impressed upon me that I cannot take the money given to preach the gospel—and maintain the homes and regular ministries of the Enterprises—and use it in a libel suit. It would violate the conscience of some, and it could get us in trouble with the Internal Revenue Service. Therefore, this will have to be a personal matter."

This was not something he entered into without much thought and prayer. "I believe this is necessary for the reopening of the homes and for the protection of such homes and churches in the future. I believe this fight has brought about a new respect for the ministry and preachers of the gospel."

This action was not without biblical precedent. The old prophet said, "When we cease to spoil, we'll be spoiled." Lester reminded our faithful friends that God permitted the Israelite woman to take jewelry away from the Egyptian women. Armies lived off the spoil from their victories over the enemy. King Uzziah was told by Azariah, the preacher, along with eighty other preachers, to get out of the temple; in other words, the state was told to get out of the church.

"We must rebuild the image of all of our ministries and take fear out of the hearts of the parents who desperately need a place to send their children."

41

Death Row for the Homes Again

By March, 1975, the Texas Welfare Department had filed against my husband again for contempt and for being in violation of their rules and regulations.

We had built up to two hundred girls—half of what we had before—at the Rebekah Home. We turned away three thousand while we were gradually taking back those two hundred. And then we found ourselves again on what my husband called "death row."

The Welfare Department was determined to take away the sixteen- and seventeen-year-olds. If they succeeded, it meant we would close down and that would be the death of the Enterprises' work. But my husband saw it not just as a battle for the Enterprises. "This is God's battle," he emphasized, as he pointed us all to Psalm 2 and then to Acts 4:25 and 26 where that writer makes mention of David's Psalm. "Who by the mouth of thy servant David hast said, Why did the heather rage, and the people imagine vain things? The kings of the earth stood up, and the rulers were gathered together against the Lord, and against his Christ." Lester said:

There you are. That's who this battle is about right there. That's why the Enterprises is under pressure today. We have no message but Christ. We have no creed but

Christ. We have no deliverance except Christ.

It was Peter and John who were talking in the Acts' passage. These two men had been brought before the rulers and elders of Israel. When they were released, they were commanded to speak no more in Jesus' name nor teach about Him.

There will always be those, even among the Christian community, who will say we were stretching the point to liken our situation to that of the disciples. But we didn't see it that way, and I suspect if the critical reader had been in our shoes he might have felt differently. Lester brought to our attention what Peter and John said.

"But Peter and John answered and said unto them, Whether it be right in the sight of God to hearken unto you more than unto God, judge ye.

"For we cannot but speak the things which we have seen and heard.

"So when they had further threatened them, they let them go . . ." (Acts 4:19-21).

This is a tragedy we're facing, folks. My soul is exercised more than it has ever been in all of my life. Even though I've been some twenty days in the weakest condition, I'd like to say that my faith is stronger than it has ever been. This old body may get weak and not be as fast and active as it used to be, but thank God, I'm not breaking in faith. I believe in Jesus Christ more than I've ever believed in Him. I believe this old Bible. I may not sleep as much as I used to, but while I'm awake I'm having fellowship with the One who loved me and gave Himself for me.

And so the disciples said, "Now, Lord, behold their

threatenings . . ." (Acts 4:29). That's all I've known now for years. They've come and said, "This is our last letter; this is special delivery; this is registered; this is your last call. We're going to close the Park Avenue Christian Day School, too. Your homes are going to have to close." Threatenings—that's all we've known.

And so the disciples said, "And now, Lord, behold their threatenings; and grant unto thy servants, that with all boldness they may speak Thy Word" (v. 29).

That's the longing of my heart. People say, "Well where do we stand, Brother Roloff?" We stand exactly where little Moses stood when he was born with the death sentence over his head. And I believe that we have a proper child to protect.

I say we're right now at the place where three million Israelites were at the Red Sea—the crisis of their lives.

We stand where Esther stood . . . and Daniel stood. Unscrupulous laws have always been passed against God's children. . . .

But I'd like to say this. If I don't go *up* real soon, I'm not going to give up, and I'm not going to give in, and by the grace of God, I'm not going to give out. I believe that God said, "Occupy till I come," and that's a military term that means to take some ground and stand on it, defend it, and stay with it.

The Bible says we ought to obey God rather than men. If I were to say to the state welfare department, "You can come now and take over and I'll work with you," I would be saying that the Bible is not sufficient to run our homes, that Jesus is not the Head of the church any more, that the church does not have the manifold wisdom of God nor the keys that Jesus gave. I would be saying that the Holy Spirit is not the Administrator of the church any more and that I've lost my confidence in God and in Jesus.

The legislative bill that slipped through the Texas Senate on March 13, 1975, was clearly aimed, many people felt, at outlawing our homes and work. The bill clearly stated that children under eighteen must be placed in child-care facilities licensed by the Department of Public Welfare. Then in May, 1975, the same bill slipped through the Texas House. Newspaper headlines said: "Bill passed today that would force Roloff to get license."

In June another court order was issued whereby we would be held in further contempt if we did not allow inspection of the premises of our homes. We allowed the inspections—we had nothing to hide and the fines levied against us for failure to comply would have only added to our financial problems. Some of the girls were interviewed.

On July 4 and 5 in Dallas a great Liberty Rally was held, sponsored by the Christian Legal and Defense Organization, whose purpose is to protect pastors and churches in America. Dr. Jack Hyles and Dr. Bob Jones preached, and my husband, along with the boys and girls from our homes, sang and testified. We came away from those meetings strengthened and greatly encouraged.

42

Freedom's Last Call

The year 1976 was to go down in Roloff Enterprises' history as a decisive year. On January 1 of that year the new law went into effect, making it illegal for unlicensed homes to take in children under the age of eighteen. Because most of our work had been with children under that age, we knew we faced grave decisions.

Once again in May, 1976, District Judge James Meyers of Austin issued a temporary restraining order instructing Roloff Enterprises to allow state welfare workers to inspect the Rebekah Home for Girls in Corpus Christi, the Lighthouse for Boys on Padre Island, and the Anchor Home for Boys at Zapata. This time we refused to comply; state welfare workers were refused entrance at the Rebekah Home and the Lighthouse.

Our reason for refusing access was that we knew we were in violation of their new law and had been since January 1. And so my husband was faced with a contempt of court charge and another five-day jail sentence. We faced penalties that could range from $50 to $1,000 per facility for each day we operated without such a license.

On Thursday, June 3, a noon rally in Woolridge Park, Austin, preceded my husband's court appearance to fight the state licensing. Some four hundred people turned out to show support carrying placards proclaiming, "Let's stand behind the man that stands for God," and, "Keep the Roloff Homes open."

For two days District Judge Charles Mathews heard from tearful fathers who told of our efforts on behalf of their sons—criminal youths—who came back from their lives of crime into society as useful citizens. Each of these men said he, if he were in my husband's position, would refuse state inspection because it would violate his religious convictions.

One father, whose son was convicted of rape and had spent several months in jail before being released on probation to the Lighthouse, testified that his son was receiving the kind of help—spiritual help—that would change him.

On June 21, 1976, a large crowd of our boys and girls accompanied my husband to the Nueces County Jail. Lester calls this the "crisis event of my life." Turning to the fellows and girls, he said, "If I never come out of this jail you're worth it." Through their tears the group managed to sing: "There's something mighty sweet about the Lord, no matter what people say." Three sisters who had been caught up in dope in Chicago were among that group. One of them stepped forward as Lester walked into the elevator, and she said what must have been on the hearts of all gathered there: "Thank you, Brother Roloff, for going to jail in my place."

Just prior to entering jail, as a result of the pressure and tensions brought to bear on him, Lester was covered with hives from the top of his head to the soles of his feet. This had been followed by a severe case of the mumps. He was not well when he entered jail.

When he went in, most of us felt another writ of habeas corpus would be received, and he would be out shortly. But such was not to be the case. This time he was in for five days.

Initially he was confined in a cell along with thirty-one other prisoners, but after the first night he was moved to a single cell. He had not asked to be moved but was grateful for this act of kindness on the part of the jailer. Scores of telegrams and letters arrived while he was in jail. Many were congratulatory cards for his sixty-second birthday.

A letter I sent to my husband while in jail meant much to him. Of it he said, "When the road is rough and the task is tough, the wife usually surfaces with an encouraging word and this is what my wife wrote to me":

My sweetheart, I dreamed Sunday night that you stood by my bed crying and unable to speak. It woke me up and I wanted to see if you were all right, but you sleep so lightly and I knew you needed all the rest you could get. Now I think the Lord was letting me know that you are going through the fire for five days. I couldn't sleep last night for thinking of where you were, what you were sleeping on, the companions and all the devil's tools going full blast—enough to drive any Christian crazy—but for the Lord.

Darling, this refiner's fire is going to bring out pure gold. Only good can come through this persecution of God's preacher. My heart bleeds for you, and I would gladly take your place if I could. Truth crushed to earth simply has to rise again. To go to prison for doing good is the greatest tragedy of our time, especially when our tax dollars are supporting the sex offenders and gangsters in our national government. I love you twice as much as I ever did. I pray for you constantly, especially during the long hours of the night. May the Lord watch between thee and me while we are absent one from the other. The Lord will prevail. As the girls say, "Hang in there." Your Wife.

On June 25, three days before his birthday, my husband was released. Newspaper headlines announced: AILING ROLOFF RELEASED FROM COUNTY JAIL. This happened on the morning of the fifth day of his sentence. When he came out, he was dehydrated and had lost weight. His stomach had bothered him and so he had eaten nothing, only drinking goat's milk and buttermilk.

Asked about his jail treatment, he replied, "I have no criticism of them. I was offered kindness. I talked, preached, witnessed, and counseled." The remaining $1,250 of a $1,750 fine levied by the court was also paid.

There was a great rally at the jail when he came down the elevator. I was allowed to go up to see him first and accompany him down. It grieved me to see him look so ill, but he was praising the Lord as usual.

Throughout these years of battling with the state of Texas and the welfare department many letters have been sent to the editors of newspapers about the issue at stake. Some of these have come to our attention. Some have been in opposition to our stance, but for the most part the letters to the editor have been overwhelmingly in our favor. The Corpus Christi paper, in its September 9, 1976, issue, stated:

The following are representative of the more than 4,000 letters the *Caller* has received from supporters of Lester Roloff, in response to his appeal for an outpouring of mail. Space limitations prevent our publishing them all; if other letters present new ideas on the subject, they will be considered for publication.

Persecution

Editor, The *Caller:*

I'm writing this letter in order to appeal to you to use

the utmost of your influence to keep open the works of Rev. Lester Roloff. . . .

If there was ever a case of religious persecution in this century, it has been directed against Lester Roloff. All over America there are thousands of pastors and many more thousands of Christian lay people who are praying earnestly and watching with great interest, believing that the disposition of this case will determine whether or not the day of nationwide religious persecution has descended upon true believers in America, as it came at other times to Russia, China, Cuba and South Viet Nam when the Americans withdrew from their commitment there. . . .

BOB JONES III
(President, Bob Jones
University, Greenville, S.C.)

Comparison

Editor, The *Caller:*

May I propose an economic and moral question for your serious consideration?

Recently I read in the Dallas *Times-Herald* where it costs the state of Texas about $15,000 per year for each juvenile in its custody and this becomes even higher because of the large percentage of repeaters.

Not only does this reveal crime's economic outrage but a very poor record of definite and lasting rehabilitation of the youth under the state's jurisdiction

The question: As "Crusaders for truth and right," why don't you help get the state off the back of Lester Roloff when his track record for not just rehabilitation but for decent, upstanding, moral and useful Christian young men and women surpasses the state's best efforts so far there is no respectable comparison? Besides, it has cost Texas taxpayers zero dollars nor has it siphoned off any "federal" money. Rather in your city's case, the Roloff Enterprises have made a considerable economic contribution. . . .

DR. ART WILSON
(Springfield, Mo.)

One voice

Editor, The *Caller:*

Since I'm from Plains, Ga., and know Jimmy Carter personally, I was beginning to look on 1976 with a very optimistic eye.

Then suddenly I hear the Texas government is once again attempting to put the "tights" on a great Christian work there in your very town. This coming at a time when I thought the Christian attitude rather than government controls was gaining momentum.

I do trust The *Caller* realizes the importance for successful work to be "left alone" in order to get the job done.

Yes, I realize I am but one small voice far removed from the political scene there in Texas but in the name of rightness I rise in support of the entire work of the Roloff Evangelistic Enterprises. . . .

C. LOGAN BUCHANAN
(Plains, Ga.)

Adds protest

Editor, The *Caller:*

Knowing you are entirely familiar with all the aspects of the state welfare department's interference in the ministry of Brother Lester Roloff, I simply wish to add my protest to the thousands of others you are receiving

229

from freedom-loving Americans who object to the Communistic tactics of the state against a wonderful work such as this.

Whatever your personal opinion of Brother Roloff, if you had the interest of boys and girls at heart, you could use your pen to help keep these homes open and I am asking that you weigh carefully your responsibility in this case, according to what is right and just. Thus far you have used your paper only to tear down this mighty work, which is God's work. God have mercy on you.

MARTHA M. GREEN

Wrong side

Editor, The *Caller:*

We are fairly new to Corpus Christi, having lived here only a year and a half; and we are sorely disappointed in your newspaper. Having lived in Tennessee, Georgia, the Rio Grande Valley and Corpus Christi, and having subscribed to the local newspaper in each respective location, we believe The *Caller* is the most inferior, one-sided newspaper ever to come into our home.

In every article of controversial nature, you take the side which is opposite of morality and decency. . . . The articles, in which you must condone homosexuality, a nudist colony, topless bathing and the biased reporting against Brother Roloff, are examples of just a few. It seems to us that you are bent on perpetrating upon your readers the philosophy that it is no longer relevant to be morally upright or to follow the code of conduct set forth in the Bible which is the Word of God. The thing that bothers us most is the fact that you do not seem to be satisfied with just being a reprobate yourself, or at least siding with them to advance their philosophy, but you would tie the hands of those who would like to be something different. If that is not true, why would you be against giving boys and girls who are in trouble or on drugs the chance to get their lives straightened out by meeting the Lord Jesus Christ in one of Brother Roloff's homes? . . .

JOHN T. BRYANT JR.

I, too, sent a letter to the Corpus Christ paper, and it was printed along with the others:

Please help

Editor, The *Caller:*

My name is Mrs. Lester Roloff. I am writing you on behalf of my dear husband who faces another court hearing in Austin, on Sept. 13, resulting possibly in closing our three homes, a long jail sentence for my husband, and another large fine.

Surely you can realize how important our work is here in Corpus Christi where we have lived for 30 years. In the first place, we contribute to the city's business approximately $1 million a year. This is not ours personally but what the Roloff Evangelistic Enterprises and the radio listeners contribute to a carrying on of our work. Do the people of Corpus Christi wish to lose that profit? In the second place, we do not take any tax funds from the state or national government for the maintenance of our homes. In the third place, we could never turn away boys and girls who could not obtain help in any of our state institutions for they, in the majority of cases, have been dope addicts and have criminal records. So where are our 400 children to go? On the streets? To the bordello? To the bars and hippie hives?

Isn't there something that the people of Corpus Christi can do? All we ask is to be able to run our homes as Christian homes, closely tied to our church, to God's Word—the Bible, and to the Lord Jesus Christ above all. Our U.S. Constitution gives us the right to worship as we please and according to the dictates of our own hearts.

We are supposed to be protected under our federal Constitution from invasion of privacy. We are supposed to have freedom of religion and freedom of speech. We are supposed to be innocent until proven guilty. We have had none of these protections—mainly because of false reports in magazines, newspapers, and gossip of little girls who lied and have since retracted their stories.

Can't you, won't you please do something to help my dear husband? He and I are no longer young. He is 62 and I am 62. We have so little time left in order to help as many people as we can.

People of Corpus Christi, please wake up and help us.
MARIE B. ROLOFF

The battle was intensified through the courts during the fall months of 1976. Attorney General John Hill arranged to meet my husband at the Rebekah Home and asked him for a personal tour, which was arranged. Before coming the Attorney General was quoted by the Corpus Christi *Times* as stating that he was encouraging my husband to continue his legal action to the U.S. Supreme Court. At the same time, however, Hill stated that we must follow the law as it now stands. "He can't ignore it pending appeal. I would like to see if there is some way we can resolve that. I don't have any desire to close the school. If we can be reasonable with each other, we may be able to come to an agreement that would have them comply on a voluntary basis until the issue is litigated. We cannot ignore the basic regulations in the meantime. It is not something that I can appropriately ignore as the people's lawyer."

After visiting with my husband, Hill said the Rebekah Home would "absolutely meet state standards if we would allow inspection." Hill went on the say; "I was impressed. The physical facilities were excellent. The program was good, probably one of the best I've seen."

My husband told the Attorney General: "The law is unconstitutional and accepting licensing would steal my conscience and drive me from the ministry or immediately stop the effectiveness of our work. We could close this running issue in a few weeks if I could work with the state rather than under them." My husband specifically asked the Attorney General to allow our homes to stay open just as they were, unlicensed, until a final test of the question of separation of church and state could be resolved by the Supreme Court.

During these months my husband asked radio listeners and friends of the Enterprises to write letters to people in places of responsibility in our government. The voice of the people was heard as they responded in overwhelming fashion.

In November, as it came time to write his monthly *Faith Enterprise* report, Lester said, "I feel like writing this *Faith Enterprise* on my knees because of what's happened." He went on to tell of meeting once again in the Austin court:

> We walked into court, two hundred miles from where we live, in the capital city of our state, Austin, Texas, and sat by the side of five lawyers. First, we were refused a change of venue to have our case tried in our home town of Corpus Christi where we've been more than thirty-two

years. Second, we were refused a jury trial, and a summary judgment was granted the welfare department which put a $23,500 fine on the Enterprises for obeying the Lord because, according to them, we were disobedient to the statute of the state. We were placed under a twenty-five thousand dollar bond.

Now, that may seem bad, but the greatest thing was that the judge was kind enough to recommend that we stay open while in litigation, and the state lawyers and the welfare lawyers were kind enough to permit it. The twenty-five thousand dollar bond is a supersedes bond which means it supersedes all charges and gives us freedom to operate on the way to the Supreme Court of the United States. The fine does not have to be paid unless and until the highest court in the land declares that the statute is constitutional and the state has a right to operate and set standards for a church home.

I feel more free today than I've felt in more than three years. We got in the plane and came back to Corpus, and the television cameras were waiting and so was the *Caller-Times* representative. The *Caller-Times* said, "Brother Roloff, it has been a long old hard battle. Have you thought about closing your homes and quitting?" I stood as tall as I've ever stood in my life, and with all the conviction of my soul I said "Do you have a family?" He said, "Yes, sir." I said, "Have you thought about closing your home and putting your children in the street?" To which he said meekly, "No, sir." I said, "Then we have three hundred times more than you do, and we're not about to close our homes but plan to fight on to the highest court in the land for our God-given protection under the Constitution and also the wonderful Word of God."

On a television station in Austin the interviewer asked us, "Brother Roloff, if you had the choice of closing your homes or taking a license, what would you do?" And I said, "I'd close my homes because my conscience is worth more than any project I've ever tackled no matter how wonderful."

In the thick of the battle the commanding officer asked a drummer boy to beat a retreat, and the little fellow looked puzzled and said, "Sir, I don't know how to beat a retreat, but I can beat an advance that would make the soldiers' hair stand straight on their heads."

For one hour yesterday, with nearly a hundred workers, I sounded the greatest advance we've ever known in the history of the Enterprises. I'm so tired of saying, "Not now," "Call me back later," or "Wait till after our next hearing in the court." For weeks now I've heard God's command, "Don't park here." I've driven through and around more parking lots the last three years of my life than ever before. The state welfare department waved their license and said, "You'll have to park here." But the Lord said, "Don't park here."

I've been sentenced to jail three times and been to jail two times, and the Lord said, "Don't park here." Some preachers and many friends have said, "Brother Roloff, why don't you just go the second mile and come under?" and the Lord said, "Don't park here." It wouldn't have been the second mile—it would have been the end of the trail for a God-given ministry.

People said to me more than three years ago, "Nobody has ever bucked the welfare department. You cannot buck the news media and religion and survive." Jesus walked into the cemetery at Bethany and said, "Lazarus, come forth," In other words, "Don't park here." And he came

235

forth bound hand and foot in grave clothes, and Jesus said in effect, "Loose him and let him go. Don't let him park in the city of the dead."

The judge (God bless his heart) at the close of the tense time of our trial said, "You know, many years ago as a lawyer I tried a case (and won it) of a man who afterward became my law partner. When I won the case, it meant that his business would be ruined, his trucks would all stop, but the judge said, 'Let's let his business continue to operate under the appeal.' And his business was saved, and his case was upheld in the appellate court." And then he said, "I recommend that these homes stay open." And the attorney general's office was kind enough to let us remain open on our long expensive trip to the Supreme Court of the United States.

And I just "thanked God and took courage." How many times in this long dark night and in the old Nueces County Jail House I've thought of Paul when he said, "There stood by me this night the angel of God, whose I am, and whom I serve, Saying, 'Fear not, Paul; thou must be brought before Caesar: and, lo, God hath given thee all them that sail with thee.' Wherefore, sirs, be of good cheer: for I believe God, that it shall be even as it was told me" (Acts 27:23-25).

43

On Our Way
to the Supreme Court

We were able to finish 1976 and approach the new year of 1977 feeling that we were on our way to the Supreme Court. God has given us some probation time.

In the meantime the film of faith, *Freedom's Last Call*, has been made and is being seen in churches across the land. The film is dedicated to the finishing of our fight through the courts and to the construction of buildings and the enlargement of all the ministries.

Even at this writing a new dormitory for the boys is being built. This time, however, it is being built in Corpus Christi on the Enterprises' farm. This will allow us to work more closely with the boys and will also allow them to participate more fully in the great services we have at the People's Church.

My husband said, "We've been at the whipping post for more than three years—the whipping post of newspapers, magazines, television, the welfare department, and religion. But with His stripes we've been healed, and I believe our work is being healed, and I'm sounding this as the greatest advance in the history of the Enterprises.

"Oh, I feel like 'a bird out of prison' that our girls sing so often, and this fresh breath of freedom's air causes my heart to rejoice. As I walked out of the courthouse, I said as Mary, the mother of our Lord once said, 'My soul doth magnify the Lord' "

Wherever my husband goes these days, he pleads with people to pray that the Lord will bring America back under Old Glory with liberty and justice for all. He tells the story of a great mountain climber who died in an effort to reach the top of a mountain. When Lester relates this story, he says, *"He died climbing.* May the day never come when we'll lose our desire to climb higher into heavenly things."

Someone once said to Lester Roloff: "Do you ever feel like saying, 'Will there never be any end to the needs and to the cry for help?' "

My husband, as usual, had a reply. "Yes, when there are no more souls to save, no more fallen girls to pick up, no more drunkards to rescue, no more dope addicts to point to the Lord, and no more homeless boys to keep out of jails, penitentiaries, and reform schools."

On November 1, 1977, a great "Save Our Nation" freedom rally was held at the convention center in Dallas, Texas. People came from across the country to fill the center. Included in that vast crowd were over 1,500 preachers who were willing to testify with my husband in this fight to maintain the separation of church and state. He urged them to continue to claim 2 Samuel 23:12, "But he stood in the midst of the ground, and defended it . . . and the Lord wrought a great victory."

Among those participating in the evening's program and sitting on the platform were Dr. Bob Jones, Jr., and Dr. Bob Jones, III, from Bob Jones University; Dr. Jack Hyles; Lt. Clebe McClary; and Dr. Bob Gray. The combined choirs from the homes sang, and the dramatic but tragic story of Uzziah the king was reenacted (2 Chron. 26:16-21). Against the protests of Azariah, the priest, the king entered the temple to offer incense (a job only the priests were allowed to do). For his disobedience he was smitten with leprosy and thrust out by the prophets, and he remained a leper for the balance of his life.

My husband followed this by once again calling upon the Christians in this nation to stand with him as his battle with the state of Texas continues and as he awaits the opportunity to present his case to the highest court in the land.

Epilogue

On Sunday, August 17, 1975, the Corpus Christi *Caller-Times* began a series of articles concerning my husband and his work. The reporters visited all of the homes operated by the Roloff Evangelistic Enterprises. My husband flew with them in the plane so they could cover all the ground in a short space of time. Then they wrote their series of six articles. The articles were under the heading, "The Rev. Lester Roloff: A to Z."

Those articles, though containing some pertinent facts about my husband and his labors for the Lord, were unsympathetic to the work. This led me to write my own version of "Brother Roloff: A to Z." I left it where he would see it when he returned home. My husband sent it to the editor, and it appeared in the *Caller* on Thursday, September 11, 1975. The article reads as follows:

Editor, the *Caller:*

I am sorry for the unkind things that have been said about my husband in the Roloff A to Z articles and some of the letters that have followed. After having known him for 40 years and being married to him for over 39 years, I would like to give you my A to Z observations of his life.

He has always been:

A-biding in Christ to meet every need
B-elieving the Bible from cover to cover
C-onquering the temptations by the devil
D-elivering the message the Holy Spirit gives
E-ndeavoring to help those who are down and out
F-orgiving even his enemies and those who betray

friendship

G-oing, even when tired and ill, to preach the Word

H-aving the courage to follow his convictions

I-nsistently urging his workers to do their best

J-esus is ALL in all

K-eeping the message that he preaches to others

L-oving the unlovely

M-ounting up with wings as an eagle

N-eeding spiritual strength to keep going

O-ffering free salvation from Christ

P-raying continually for others

Q-uesting for the lost to be saved

R-esting on every Bible promise

S-erving others through six homes and preaching the gospel

T-rusting the Lord to meet every need

U-nderstanding the problems of drug addicts and others in need

V-aluing friendships made through the ministry

W-aiting on the Lord to renew his strength

X-raying the lying coverups of those he helps

Y-earning toward those he cannot take—no room

Z-ealously defending the faith

All of these may be summed up in God's ABC's as given in Revelation 21:6 and 22:13.

"And he said unto me, It is done, I am Alpha and Omega, the beginning and the end. I will give unto him that is athirst of the fountain of the water of life freely."

"I am Alpha and Omega, the beginning and the end, the first and the last."

Brother Roloff's power is from Christ; to fellow Christians there is no enigma.

MRS. LESTER ROLOFF

When my husband and I were talking about this book, his only request was that in the closing chapter I give my opinion of him and his work. I think that the above letter to the editor gives an accurate summation of what I think of him. I cannot say, as some people do, that we never have had an argument. I cannot say I have always agreed with him. I cannot say he is perfect; he has his faults as I have mine. Life with Lester Roloff has not been dull.

I have presented my husband and the work God entrusted to him in an honest way. This is the true story of Lester Roloff. I hope and pray that now you understand him and the work that the Lord called him to do a little better. I trust this will encourage other preachers. He is the most dedicated and most earnest man I know. If it were August 10, 1936 again, and if he would have me, I would marry him all over again. The times have not always been easy, but as I have heard my husband say so many times, "There is a thorn on every rose, but aren't the roses sweet?" He is recognized for his unusual quotes. Another favorite goes like this: "Two men looked out of prison bars; one saw mud, the other saw stars!"

Lester Roloff has looked out of prison bars. His gaze has always been upward, to the One who created those stars.

The old Indian prayer is familiar to many, but it seems a fitting closing to what I want to say about my husband: "Great Spirit, grant that I may not criticize my neighbor until I have walked a mile in his moccasins."

I could not walk a mile in my husband's shoes. He goes too far, too often, too fast. But I can "Stay by the stuff" (I Sam. 30:24). And I pray for him. This is my role as the wife of this one I consider to be a great and godly man, but he would be the first to tell you the Lord has done it all.

Part Three

Lester Roloff — In Life And In Death
Bobby R. Glenn

44

Interlude of Hope

Given a time of reprieve as the case against him made its way to the Supreme Court of the United States, Lester Roloff enjoyed some much needed relief from the pressures of daily fines and harassment from the State Welfare Department. This gave him some time to reflect back over the long battle through the courts. Had it been worth the battle? Would he make the same decisions again if he were called upon to subjugate the work to the rules of the state? He paid a high price in the toll on his health. He was asked, "Is this work really worth that price?" Brother Roloff replied, "Hundreds of youngsters under eighteen years old have been converted to Christ during the battle with the state, and that alone makes it worthwhile. However, if the Supreme Court now rules in our favor, the doors will be wide open to continue rescuing this critical age group until Jesus comes. It will also encourage others to begin similar ministries. That is our goal."

Temporarily, the homes ministered to as many of the younger boys and girls as their facilities could accommodate. This was the agreement with the courts and the Department of Human Resources. There were no restraints on accepting those youngsters over sixteen years of age.

Each day brought new opportunities of ministering to so many who were hurting. Brother Roloff welcomed the increasing demand for the services of the homes. He gave God the glory and looked forward to a great harvest of souls being rescued from their headlong and helpless plunge into the flames of Hell. In January, 1978, Brother Roloff wrote:

> We have just baptized seventy-six of the happiest converts I have ever seen, but, oh, what they looked like and acted like when they came in! A daddy stood to his feet (during the service) and said, "My daughter would be in a state institution had it not been for the Rebekah Home. . . ." Our girls all applauded when he got through with his message of gratitude.
>
> Now I have promised the Lord that I will seek to rebuild and renew my mental, physical, and spiritual life during the next twelve months. According to the doctors, it is a must!

Things were going well at the homes. Wiley and Fay Cameron moved back into the Rebekah Home as superintendents. "It is," Brother Roloff said, "a good time to regain my strength, and saturate myself in scripture." However, his time of physical and spiritual restoration came to an abrupt stop. Suddenly he was thrust into the most hectic and exhausting time of his life.

45

Bad News from Washington

Brother Roloff wrote the following report in the *Family Altar News.*

Of all the sad and bad news that ever came down a news wire, October 2, 1978, brought bad news to the parents, children, and churches, nationally and internationally, that look to our homes for help.

The Supreme Court of the United States refused to hear our appeal but chose rather to uphold the decision of the lower courts and the Supreme Court of Texas to declare our church and all churches illegal in operating church homes without a license from the Department of Human Resources (DHR).

This is the most outstanding case in over 200 years of American History. If the *Mayflower* knew what was going to take place a little over 200 years later, she would have sprung a leak.

By faith, we have made our appeal to The Highest Court — Heaven's Tribunal: God the Father, God the Son, and God the Holy Spirit. Our brief has been made ready — the King James Version. The Holy Spirit will present the facts; the Lord Jesus will hear the case; and our Heavenly Father will render the final decision!

Though we may be considered legally dead, we still

believe in the resurrection, and I promise you, my faithful friends, there will be either a rapture or a resurrection, and I also believe there is going to be a judgment; as it is written, "It is given unto man once to die and after that the judgment!"

After exhausting all state remedies, we went to the Supreme Court of the United States, and this august body of senior judges refused to hear the case, saying that it was not of sufficient importance to be a federal matter. Just what that means, I am not sure. . . . To me it ought to mean that we need to go to some court and have a fair jury trial about whether we have violated the Constitution or not. That would have settled the whole matter in the outset, and that was the first request we made in Corpus Christi over four years ago. . . . The future of the church is brighter without the state than the state's future is without the church. It was not Old Glory that raised the Christian flag with its blood stained banner. It was the Christian flag and faith in Christ that raised Old Glory with her stars and stripes. The Christians and the churches will soon be needed to come out bearing their flag again, and their illustrious past and blood-soaked heritage will help Old Glory wave again.

People sometimes quote Patrick Henry's famous response: "Give me liberty or give me death." How many really mean it? How many Americans are there with that much steel in their backbones? He said, "Is life so dear or peace so sweet as to be purchased with the chains of slavery? I know not what course others may take, but as for me, give me liberty or give me death."

46

Court Requires Licensing

It was no surprise that On May 16, 1979, Attorney General Mark White asked Judge Mathews to find Roloff in contempt of the 1976 order because he continued to run the homes without a license.

On June 14, 1979, the McAllen, Texas, *Monitor* printed an article under the heading: "Roloff Told to Seek Licensing." It read:

> Evangelist Lester Roloff has six days to decide to quit resisting attempts to license his troubled youth facilities or see his girls and boys taken away.
>
> Roloff was not present Wednesday when State District Judge Charles Mathews ordered the three homes closed unless they applied for a state license by Tuesday.
>
> When Brother Roloff heard the news, he said, "They'll hang black crepe on Heaven's gate if they close these homes. . . . My heart's aching and breaking over what happened today. . . . The license is a Russian Communist piece of equipment. There is no doubt in my mind. The license is altogether unconstitutional, illegal, historically wrong, practically wrong, and biblically wrong." Mathews also ordered Lester Roloff Evangelistic Enterprises, Inc., to pay $22,850. in civil penalties.
>
> (Attorney General) White and Governor Bill Clements visited the Rebekah Home on April 11. Both were quite vocal in their praise for the excellent facilities. The governor later vowed to find a solution to Roloff's

problems with the state welfare department.

Sunday, before the fateful Tuesday deadline, an article from the Associated Press wire reported:

Evangelist Lester Roloff is preparing for what may be the last battle in his six-year legal war with the state.

Brother Roloff had this to say about the court order: "When they put a license on the church, they put a license on the pastor."

He reiterated his claim that Tuesday will be remembered as a big day in American history. "Tuesday will write the story of another Alamo," he said from the pulpit.

"Any thoughts of violence will be put to rest. There will be none," he said. "The heavier the burden, the more you ought to sing. It confuses the devil."

He said the court order that may close the homes is "murder for the hopes of these young people." There were about 400 youths in the homes.

And despite the possibility that the children will be taken from here Tuesday and the chance that he will be jailed, Roloff talked of long-range plans.

47

Final Orders: Close Homes!

An AP news release on June 20, 1979, describes the death knell issued by state officials. It read:

A state welfare official and the head of the Department of Public Safety (DPS) intelligence division obtained final orders today to close Evangelist Lester Roloff's youth homes.

State District Judge Charles Mathews of Austin gave welfare workers the go-ahead to remove children from the Rebekah Home for Girls and the Lighthouse Home for Boys.

Marlin Johnston, associate commissioner of the Texas Department of Human Resources, and Capt. Hugh Pogue flew from Austin to deliver certified copies of Mathews' order.

About 100 staff members of Human Resources Department were massed near Corpus Christi, awaiting the order's arrival.

Plans call for the young people to be returned to their parents or placed in (state) foster homes.

Johnston said, "We have to play it by ear, step by step."

"A Diary from Rebekah" was written daily by Miss Ida Cavitt from the perspective of a girl ordered removed from the Home. The diary detailed the actions of the ministry and the actions of the DHR and DPS. The following are excerpts from the diary Wednesday, June 20, 1979:

By three o'clock P.M. the People's Church was nearly full of preachers, parents, church members, and interested friends from Corpus Christi. Brother Roloff instructed everyone to maintain a sweet Christian attitude and requested that no one speak an unkind word to the members of the DHR or the Department of Public Safety who came along to assist them. He also asked everyone to follow the leadership of Dr. Gregg Dixon and Dr. Earl Little whom he had appointed "Captains," and he called them his "Travis and Bowie" of the "Rebekah Alamo of Christian Liberty."

Dr. Dixon then introduced Attorney David Gibbs who very solemnly told everyone in the auditorium, "You must understand that when you go outside this church building and stand in the line, you will be subject to arrest and you can be taken to jail. If you resist an officer, you can immediately be arrested. If you have children in this auditorium, though they are not in the homes, those children can be picked up along with the Rebekah girls. I want you to understand this, and if you choose to leave now, you may be excused."

Then Dr. Dixon gave the following instructions:

"The preachers will form the first line of defense around the entrance of the building. They will hold the American flag and the Christian flag. They will also hold their Bibles between them. Standing behind them, a row of parents of the Rebekah girls will hold their Bibles between them. Church members will comprise the next row with each of you holding your Bible between you and the person standing next to you. If DHR or DPS workers break through your line, they must knock the Bible out of your hand."

"We want them not only to have to come through the Bible but through the American and Texas flags," an unidentified man told the crowd as a large group of reporters stood by. These reporters had been expecting a violent confrontation. They must have been disappointed when they heard Brother Roloff's instructions squelching even unkindness. The Rebekah Diary continues:

He (Dr. Dixon) also told us that behind the line of church members Brother Roloff would stand in front of the locked church door. If they came through the lines, they would have to push Brother Roloff aside and break down the church door to get inside. Once they got inside, they would interrupt a church service where we girls were, and if they got any of us, it would require them to bodily pick us up as we kneeled at the altar.

I'm sure I would have been kneeling at the altar when they came in. I would have been praying for Brother Roloff and all those other people outside. They had all gone out there, even after they heard what Dr. Gibbs said. They were willing to go to jail for us; I just wanted to thank the Lord that they cared that much for us.

The sky was dark blue, made bluer by the many white clouds that drifted overhead. The Texas June sun was extremely hot. Those with fair skin stood out because of sunburn. Many were perspiring, but no one was leaving. The diary continues:

Pastors and others joined hands, raised the flag, clenched their Bibles and stood in front of the People's Church.

251

. . . The Rebekah Home is next door. Its doorknob was removed Tuesday (yesterday).

At 3:30 P.M. everyone was in place in front of the church — the preachers, the parents, and all the people. They held their Bibles and sang. A helicopter flew over the church. Everyone continued to stand and sing. Brother Roloff and Lt. Clebe McClary walked by, on their way to the Welcome Center at the entrance of the property. Lt. McClary wanted to stand in the driveway and hold the American flag. They would have to move him or run over him to get onto the church property. About 4:30 P.M. everyone was asked to come back into the church to cool off and wait until we had definite word that the DHR was on its way.

The Family Altar radio program began broadcasting live from the auditorium at 5:00 P.M. Immediately at the close of the broadcast, the word came, "They are three minutes away!" Everyone went back outside — the preachers, the parents, and the church members — and got in their places again, singing and holding their Bibles. A couple of DHR vehicles approached the entrance to the property and then passed on by.

Meanwhile someone contacted the Governor and told him what was happening. He called back and left word that he had instructed the DHR and the DPS not to break through any human barriers and not to break down any church doors.

Everyone was dismissed until church time tonight.

The daily verse in the diary was: "Touch not mine anointed, and do my prophets no harm" (Psalm 105:15).

Surprisingly, the task force of law enforcement officers did not make their move Wednesday.

Thursday, June 21, "The Diary of Rebekah" recorded a

false alarm at 6:15 in the morning. The live broadcast began at 7:00 A.M. There was another false alarm later in the morning. The day was mostly uneventful. The following note was recorded at the end of the day:

Tonight, after the services, and after Brother Roloff preached one of the best messages I ever heard him preach, the decision was made for the Rebekah girls to sleep in the church. The preachers divided into two groups, and each group is spending half the night here. They are outside now, under the stars, singing and praying. I'm sure they are praying for us as we are here inside preparing to go to sleep. I know the Lord will bless them for this; they are enjoying themselves and the sweet fellowship out there. My verse for today is: "Behold how good and how pleasant it is for brethren to dwell together in unity!" (Psalm 133:1).

On June 22, 1979, another AP release read:

The stalemated siege at Lester Roloff's Rebekah Home for Girls entered its third day today with a state task force awaiting word on its next move. One hundred girls from the Rebekah Home spent the night in the church; they slept with blankets and pillows on padded pews.

The Rev. Earl Little of Garland, one of Roloff's supporters, said the girls were moved into the church because they thought the state might come and get them during the night.

A trickling of parents coming to take their children out of the home continued during the standoff between the state and Roloff.

The 140 member state task force remains headquartered at Texas A&I University at Kingsville. While Johnston maintains the task force is not an army, he has started to talk about strategy and maneuvers.

Johnston was asked if the task force would wait until nightfall in an effort to catch the girls outside the church.

"My desire would be never to go in the middle of the night, but I wouldn't rule out anything," he said.

Once during the stalemate, the task force moved to an agency office nearby.

Mr. Johnston was the first to make a move. He arrived at the front gate and was courteously greeted by Lester Roloff and escorted in a car past the blockade into Roloff's private home. The men talked for about 20 minutes. As Johnston departed, he said he planned to talk with Brother Roloff later in the day.

48

Strategic Withdrawal

At midday Friday, June 22, State Attorney General Mark White headed to Corpus Christi for a talk with Brother Roloff. It was at that session a deal was carved out. The agreement was that Brother Roloff move the girls out of the Rebekah Home. However, he, not the state, would handle the placing of the girls; they would be moved to non-state homes temporarily. The homes would be closed, and the ministry would be restructured so that the homes would be under the People's Baptist Church, after which the girls would be returned. Dr. Gregg Dixon explained to the preachers that this was not a compromise. "This is a strategic withdrawal so you can fight another day." The state insisted on the closing of the Rebekah Home according to the court order.

Under the new system, all of the homes would operate under the aegis of the People's Baptist Church. "If the state tries to control (the homes), they would be trying to control the church," Brother Roloff said.

He thanked the preachers, prayed over them, and dismissed them so they could be in their pulpits the coming Sunday.

After that Friday night of June 22, Brother Roloff went through withdrawal fatigue. "I believe I could not have physically gone through another week," he said, "though our preachers were determined to stay. Thank God the line held!"

In reviewing the showdown, Brother Roloff said, "Our

final line of defense was the great prayer warriors who prayed and wept as they received news from the battlefront. We got calls from as far away as Australia. . . . Though weary from the long battle and from the terrible tension of that week, my heart is encouraged, my faith strong. God used my tears to make telescopes to give me a better vision of the greatness of God and the loyalty and love of our preachers and other friends."

49

Back in Business

The UPI dateline was from Corpus Christi, Texas, Friday, Sept 14. The article headline was "Roloff Back in Juvenile Rehabilitation Business." It read:

The Rev. Lester Roloff is in the juvenile rehabilitation business again, and this time he says the state must sue the People's Baptist Church to close him down.

The Evangelist, whose nonprofit corporation took a six-year battle against state licensing to the U.S. Supreme Court and lost, Thursday reopened one of his court-closed, child-care centers.

The 65-year-old fundamentalist preacher told UPI that since 180 girls left the Rebekah Home on June 25, his Roloff Evangelistic Enterprises, Inc., had placed the homes under the People's Baptist Church.

"We just rearranged everything so that if there was to be a suit, it would have to be against the church," said Roloff, who went to jail twice and was assessed $55,000. in fines for refusing to license his facilities for troubled boys and girls.

Three Roloff homes contained up to 400 children before state courts ordered them licensed or closed.

Roloff was awaiting the arrival of 50 girls from a Roloff home in Georgia where they were taken in June after Roloff and a group of *Bible-toting* (media's derogatory cliché) preachers linked to keep Texas Department of Human Resources workers from forcibly taking them from the chapel of the Roloff complex near Corpus Christi.

Roloff takes no money for rehabilitating children addicted to alcohol and drugs or in trouble with law enforcement authorities, instead operating his child-care facilities with donations from listeners to his religious broadcasts.

While the homes were being reorganized under the church, Brother Roloff kicked off the largest building campaign in the history of the ministry. There was a need to move the Anchor Home for Boys to Corpus Christi from Zapata, Texas. There was also a need to build a City of Refuge dormitory and enlarge all of the homes because of the expectation that the work would expand quickly as friends saw the opportunities and helped get under the financial load.

"People ask me what keeps me going after six years. It is the assurance that I am right — and the blessing of God," Brother Roloff said.

He asked a group of attorneys in Austin, "Who do you get your orders from — the law or the Lord? I get my orders from the Lord, and He says to go forward and reach more people."

Brother Roloff said, "We are now filing Chapter Eleven." His reference was to chapter eleven of Hebrews. This is the great chapter on living by faith.

An AP release in October of 1979 under the headline, "Roloff, State Battle Resumes," read:

Attorney General Mark White has reopened the state's longstanding feud with Evangelist Lester Roloff by suing once more to impose state child-care standards on Roloff's children's homes.

The Rebekah Home recently reopened under the auspices of Roloff's People's Baptist Church in Corpus Christi.

Roloff closed the homes this summer rather than obey a court order that he obtain licenses for them from the Texas Department of Human Resources.

Brother Roloff retained Mr. William Ball to handle the case. He was the constitutional lawyer who had earlier won before the U.S. Supreme Court for the Amish people who did not want their children forced to go to public schools.

"The legal future of the work is in the hands of the most capable constitutional lawyer alive in the world today," Brother Roloff said. (Mr. Ball was already at work, and the case was already on appeal.) "Once we get the judges and the courts back to the law of the land (the *Constitution*), which is built on the law of the Lord (the Word of God), victory will be ours."

50

Ominous Clouds

The case against the Roloff Enterprises attracted much attention across the nation during the long years of battle. There was no question as to the bias of the news media. They received little tidbits of information about what some unhappy girl or boy had said to the DHR representatives. There was a move on to get public sentiment against the homes.

Scandalous articles appeared in magazines, tabloids, and newspapers all across the nation. Many of those articles were based on a report from some rebellious girls who ran away from the homes. They gave their story to the DHR and alleged physical abuse at the Rebekah Home.

What did the media do with the report from four rebellious girls whose record would make anything they said suspect? Even after this report was firmly denied by the administrators of the homes, the report was flashed across television screens and newspaper headlines all over America.

After they milked that report of all of its destruction, they decided to check the validity of the story. Now the great fairness of the media began shining forth. They wanted to print the ministry's side of the story. "We have come to help you," should be the most feared words in America when it comes from the mouths of the news media or the government. "What a different nation we would have if the media fought as hard for freedom of religion as they do for freedom of the press," Brother Roloff remarked, "both are equally guaranteed by the Constitution." Somehow the media thinks that freedom of the press is etched a little deeper and is in no way interrelated with freedom of religion. They do not understand world history.

Like his grandfather, Lester Roloff trusted what people told him. It cost both of the men thousands of dollars, but neither wanted to give up faith in his fellow man. The news media almost cured Lester from trusting anyone. However, again he took them at their word and believed they really meant what they said. Since there was nothing to hide, he granted their request to interview him and some of his workers from the homes. Almost everything said was again twisted, distorted, and falsified as they continued to spread their poison to the nation.

Many young people wanted to testify truthfully about the homes and the personnel of the homes. The news media were not interested in the glowing reports of salvation and changed lives. They were not interested in reports that discipline was lovingly administered; they did not want to hear the girls say they were treated better and with more love than ever before. This is not sensational. Brother Roloff aptly called media reporters "Dirt Dobbers."

The girls who gave the original false reports came back, admitted their lies, and wanted back in the homes. It is ludicrous that an honest reporter would refuse to correct the injustice and recant his story. News stories are rarely, if ever, recanted other than for transposed names or wrong pictures. Innocent people are left vulnerable as the news media propagates their exposés that are not verifiable. Since these stories and articles are never recanted, it means they are always accurate in their reporting — or they are dishonest. Recanting is harmful to their image, so they just let their untruthful reports stand as if the truth were not known.

This is what the ministry had dealt with for years. Now it

was having bad effects. The contributions to the ministry from across the nation were decreasing.

Only one major documentary on national T.V. even approached objectivity; that was the program "60 Minutes." They produced two reports during the battle. Most of their statements were reliable representations of the ministry. What has happened to objectivity in the field of journalism in America? Brother Roloff said that the godless news and entertainment media have done more to destroy the moral fiber of this nation than all other evil forces combined.

Each month the same report came from the office workers — the finances would not support the needed expansion. If things did not change soon, the operations of the homes would have to be scaled back. Many more now were turned away because there was no more room; the homes were operating above capacity, and there was not enough money to pay the bills. The attorney fees and other legal expenses had drained the work, with no relief in sight. The negative nationwide coverage by the media was apparently believed by many regular supporters. "How can we continue to turn away the thousands who are applying for help through the homes every month?" Brother Roloff asked as he wept. This was the burden of his heart.

An article in the *Corpus Christi Caller Times* in June, 1980, was under the heading "Roloff Is $2 Million in the Red."

These pressures were beginning to show on the weary preacher. His eyes were sunken and tired. Much of the sparkle was gone. He was often seen massaging the muscles between his neck and shoulders while he was preaching. How could he drive himself further? He knew it would be humanly impossible to regain the trust and confidence of many former supporters of the work since some of them, without a doubt, believed the false reports that had been spread by the media.

There was no way out; Brother Roloff's time and efforts were required — fighting to keep the expenses paid for groceries, utilities, medical needs, salaries, and maintenance. The drain was incredible on him; it affected every area of the work as expenses had to be reduced. However, he was quick to inform everyone that there was no turning back. The fire of determination again lightened his eyes as he said, "Living by faith is how we started. Once you see God's provisions, you dare not go back to living by sight."

The facts were clear that the enemies of the work were gaining in the battle to close the homes. On the other hand, the homes were possibly on the verge of final victory over the state.

Fifty young people were turned away daily. This was the most disappointing thing that could happen at this time. Some asked, "Why not send them to another facility that has the same kind of ministry?" There was no similar ministry in the nation. No charge was made to those who came to the homes. Most who came were penniless when they arrived. These were youngsters who had been into deep sin and crime. Most other youth homes did not want their ilk. Judges from across the nation specifically paroled many youngsters to the Roloff Homes. Only God knows the devastation that was being inflicted on the youths who were turned away; some had no further offer of help before their lives were snuffed out by their own hands or by the hands of their scruffy associates. Brother Roloff asked his listeners to pray that God would have mercy on the souls of those who made it their business to harm the ministries. He made it clear he wanted to see them saved.

Literally buckets of tears were shed by desperate parents as they begged Brother Roloff to take their children. Day and night the calls came. Even employees of the DHR were asking him to take their children. The facilities were full, and the expenses were mounting. Turning the hordes of youngsters away kept the workers' emotions on edge; tears flowed quickly as the staff sensed the hopelessness of those who were turned away. God kept the workers from debilitating depression, but He allowed the Christian tears of compassion to flow. God's omnipotence is the only explanation for the extraordinary strength given to Brother Roloff. Wiley Cameron carried as much of the leadership role as was humanly possible. Other home leaders had their shoulders to the wheel. The large Roloff complex was straining because it was operating over capacity. God was blessing the tremendous efforts of the entire staff. Many were saved and delivered from lives of sin.

Added to the responsibility on Brother Roloff's shoulders were the "Honey Bee Quartet" and the "Jubilee Trio" who spent many hours flying with him to meetings across the country. These groups were composed of daughters of the workers and girls who had received help from the homes. This was a moving dimension to Brother Roloff's presentation of the work. People saw and heard firsthand some undeniable results of the work as the girls sang and gave their personal testimonies. It was not unusual to see those in the congregations weeping at the testimonies of God's unspeakable mercy and grace. Some parents wept because the testimonies echoed their painful personal experiences with their own daughters or sons. Youngsters wept because what the girls said described the dilemma in which they presently found themselves. The chords of Christian compassion within hearts began to vibrate again. Tangible help resulted as churches responded.

Brother Roloff alone carried the burden of getting his precious cargo safely to their appointments in widely separated churches and auditoriums. This required some night flying, and sometimes it was necessary to fly in weather conditions that were not ideal.

How would he get the true message to the churches and other supporters fast enough to prevent a scaling back of the work? His plan, dictated by necessity, was to use this time while the appeal was making its way to the Supreme Court as a time of raising support rather than a time for obtaining the critically needed rest and restoration. He would have to do extensive traveling. Many asked, "Why would the Lord allow this man to be driven to the breaking point after what he had been through?" Questioning the Lord was not part of Brother Roloff's style; no one ever heard him accusing God.

He remembered those dear Christians who, as has already been reported, would say, "Brother Roloff, I'd rather you burn at the stake than to bend or to bow or to compromise. The Christian world is watching to see if you will stand." He did not cringe from being a martyr for Christ. However, working himself to death raising funds to rescue hundreds and thousands of society's outcasts was not as challenging to him as preaching himself to death while seeing the Holy Spirit turning their lives around. But, it was necessary, and, if that is what God wanted from him, he would give himself in obedience.

His determination was growing stronger. There were those who believed that he sensed the remainder of his life would be spent and sacrificed for the debauched, degenerated, and depraved. Rather than being discouraged about the prospects of this revelation, if indeed there was one, he seemed to have crossed a threshold into a room where he sampled the air from another world. The fires of conviction flashed anew from his blue eyes. In June, 1980, he said, "You can't change what is right; you can't change God. I'd rot in somebody's jail before I would take a license." More than America's youth were involved. There were those from other countries. He had made trips to the West Indies and the Virgin Islands in evangelistic meetings. Many of those people realized they had been visited by one of God's noblemen. As a result, several black youths from the islands were in the homes.

Apparently he was beginning to see that giving his life would be preferred to trading his God-given convictions for a mess of state pottage.

Our great Constitution's Christian liberties, bought at such high costs, were now being challenged just as they would be in totalitarian countries. There would be no reviving of this particular religious freedom in America if this case failed. He would have to see this case through the Supreme Court of the United States. If he failed there — he would continue to obey God and accept the consequences.

Increasing numbers of homosexuals and atheists were already making their way into the state and federal government and into regulatory jobs. They realized any youth work that used the Bible in its program was detrimental to their cause. The reason for this is that the Bible condemns their sins. How depressing to the preacher were the prospects of seeing people with that warped mentality accepted and allowed to have any authority over churches and their ministries. Those people are rightly projects for church ministries. The preacher's comments on decaying government and pervert favored regulations upheld by godless justices would be remembered and repeated often in the years that followed.

To Brother Roloff it would be easier to die than to see the churches brought under government control. Churches can go underground and many have been forced to do that in other countries. They chose to operate unlawfully rather than to submit to government controls. Consequently, they were condemned by the government and the religious hierarchy — but they were blessed by God. How could that happen in America? "How many brave American Christians have already given their lives for that liberty?" Brother Roloff asked. "How many courageous soldiers have given life and limb to preserve that freedom? I will not give up such a costly legacy."

How can America's Christians stand by quietly as this blood-written constitutional guarantee is made useless? Lester Roloff never lost his appreciation for this glorious document? Will American Christians be guiltless when they stand before the One who inspired it and gave it into their trust? The blood of their forefathers will cry out from the ground on which they died. America was settled largely by those who were fleeing church compromise, government meddling in the church, regulation, and persecution. God provided a place where they could worship Him unmolested. They educated their children according to their convictions, evangelized, carried on church ministries for those in need, read the Bible, and prayed wherever and whenever they pleased. Brother Roloff believed those rights were being "methodically taken from Americans," and there was no vigorous resistance. Americans elected leaders without asking where they stood on Christian liberties; those liberal leaders, in turn, appointed their own kind to the Supreme Court, and more Christian guarantees were struck down. The cycle continued; nothing much was said because people wanted peace. But, a nation's peace has always depended on God and the freedom to worship and serve Him. He makes it clear that He will not bless a nation which does not obey Him.

Lester Roloff said, "When it becomes unlawful to worship and obey God, the true Christians will be lawbreakers."

Were Lester Roloff's comments of not bowing to the god of government just bold rhetoric and bravado? He must have reflected back often on what the costs had already been. *I was sentenced twice to the Nueces County Jail. I have paid heavy fines. My life has been threatened. All kinds of compromises have been proposed to me. I must not waver now; my course is set; I will pay with my life before I will give up my God-given convictions.* He was accustomed to attempts to make him compromise or fall. He often said, "Anyone who takes a strong stand for the Bible and against sin will be the target of Satan and his crowd."

Once in his ministry, he received a telephone call from a young woman who told him she needed counseling and spiritual help. She asked him to come to her apartment which he agreed to do. Knowing the dangers of this type of situation, he wisely asked a young man of the church to go along. When they knocked on the door, a female voice said, "Come in." When they opened the door, the woman lay completely naked on her bed. Brother Roloff grabbed a sheet, and he and the young man with him held it up so as not to see the woman while they approached the bed. They threw the sheet over the woman. Then, after sternly reprimanding her, Brother Roloff told her they loved her in the Lord and wanted to see her saved from her sins. He presented the gospel clearly and left the spurned woman with an invitation to attend the Sunday church services.

Those kinds of attacks he had grown to expect. He kept prayed up, and God helped him handle them. But Satan now had his big guns out. The Welfare Department with an array of tax-paid attorneys at their command had drained the ministry of large sums of money. Then, with their consuming passion to "get" Roloff, they were joined by the godless news media. Together they judged him guilty. For his punishment they attacked his base of financial support.

Thinking of the formidable task of shoring up what had taken seventeen long years to build was heart rending.

Brother Roloff was surely thinking, *What if my weary body cannot take the rigors of visiting numerous churches in my attempt to regain the finances necessary to carry on the work?* What a tragedy if, at this time of potential victory, his expectations were thwarted because of physical exhaustion.

Then he would remember what Paul, through the leading of the Holy Spirit, had recorded in Philippians 1:6, "Being confident of this very thing, that he which hath begun a good work in you will perform it until the day of Jesus Christ."

The Roloff Enterprises' logo, printed in red ink on stationery and *mail-outs*, includes the following two quotes: *"Now the just shall live by faith,"* and *"Christ is the Answer."* These quotes always worked on Brother Roloff like an army bugler sounding a "charge"; they provided the impetus needed to tackle seemingly impossible projects. He was encouraged that the ministry would be getting its day in the nation's highest court; but Satan saw to it that any advances were countered by ominous dark clouds on other fronts.

Were there not other representatives who could present the ministry's needs in the churches? Yes, there were others who were willing to do their part. They traveled as much as possible. Their schedules were usually made long in advance because they also had enormous responsibilities at the homes. In the time of crisis, Brother Roloff was the only one available who could call a pastor and ask to be worked in on a particular date and usually be accommodated.

He must have longed to bring back to life his grandfather, "Uncle Billy Roloff." He would have had him pray that the Lord would meet the physical needs of his grandson and the financial needs of the ministry. How often Lester had seen the Lord meet the needs of those "Uncle Billy" prayed for when he was alive. He had one necessary thing that many Christians seem to lack — the certainty that God indeed hears their prayers and that He is interested in "anything that touches their lives." Surely Lester longed for the strength he enjoyed when his mama was alive and "prayed for her preacher-boy son every day."

Brother Roloff began pushing himself unmercifully. He flew from meeting to meeting all over the nation correcting the false charges of the DHR and the media; he challenged the people to get behind the work. Some support was salvaged, but much of it was never regained. As a result, thousands never received the help so desperately needed and wanted.

51

Political Clouds

Mark White had announced he would be seeking the office of Governor of the State of Texas. This is the man who was Attorney General and seemed to be friendly to the homes but was getting the reputation of being the "pawn" of the Welfare Department.

Brother Roloff made no bones about his opposition to Mark White becoming governor. The then present governor was Bill Clements, who publicly endorsed the program used at the homes. He later tried to use his influence to have charges dropped against Brother Roloff and the Enterprises.

During the political campaign, supporters from many states sent letters to their friends in Texas urging them to vote for Governor Clements and to support his bid for another term in office. Brother Roloff used his own finances to support Clements in every lawful way. The polls were showing that Mark White was steadily gaining on Mr. Clements. Brother Roloff was sure that God would not allow a change in the governor's office then and remarked, "It will be one of the biggest disappointments of my life if Clements is unseated."

He thought back on all of the encouragement that Governor Clements had given. He had often spoken his praise of the homes, commending their cleanliness, the excellent program and staff, and their superior facilities as compared to state homes. The predicament was not caused by the highest office in the state but by some lower elected officials. The initiative and the impetus always came from bureaucrats who wanted more power and authority over the citizens of the state. Lester Roloff explained that politicians come and go, but after every cycle the bureaucrats come out with more power.

He was concerned that parents were being judged by the DHR. Children could be removed from their parents on nothing more than an accusation. The burden was then on the parents to get their own children back and prove to the satisfaction of the bureaucrats, or courts, that they were qualified to raise them. Brother Roloff believed that of all the people in the state who should not make judgments relating to parental qualifications, it would be the DHR personnel.

52

Yet Another Step of Faith

In 1980, Ann Murphy, a missionary who had worked among the American Indians for many years, visited the Roloff Homes in Corpus Christi. She was impressed with the Christ-centered ministry that was successful in transforming alcoholics and drug addicts into responsible Christian citizens. Lester Roloff responded to the missionary's invitation to visit the reservation.

Upon seeing the desperate need among those native Americans, his conscience was stricken. "May God forgive me; I never knew this existed. We can and we must do something!"

In February of 1982, the Roloff Evangelistic Enterprises made a down payment on nearly 70 acres of land at Ft. Thomas, Arizona, and near the Apache Indian reservation. The work was not exclusively for the Apaches but for all American Indians. The dream was to eventually put Regeneration Reservations near many Indian reservations in America. This was a mission field of approximately 1.4 million Indians right here in America that was largely untouched. The first Regeneration Reservation was placed in the heart of this mission field.

The faith of Brother Roloff was clearly shown in this venture. This work was started at the apex of the financial crisis. When reminded of this fact, he said, "If the work is of God, it cannot fail."

53

The Meeting in the Air

The Christian
Sees The Invisible
Hears The Inaudible
Touches The Intangible
Believes The Incredible
Does The Impossible.
Crosses The Uncrossable
Reaches The Unreachable
Attains The Unattainable
Simply By Believing
The Promise of God

— Charlie Sharpe.

On November 1, 1982, in the McAllen, Texas, Civic Center, Evangelist Lester Roloff conducted a valley-wide crusade. He brought four choirs, quartets, and trios from the homes in Corpus Christi. Many winter Texans (those who live in colder climates but make South Texas their home in the winter months) attended the crusade. Faith Baptist Church in Mission, Texas, sponsored the event. Christians from the entire Rio Grande Valley drove to McAllen to attend the crusade.

The preacher was the usual energetic, effervescing leader as he called on one music group after another. Quartet and trio members sang and gave their testimonies. The audience responded often with resounding *Amens*. The spirit was good. The Lord was there.

Brother Roloff preached and described the work for those who were hearing him for the first time. He mentioned the heavy burden brought on by the DHR and shared with the people the financial crisis at the homes. He said, "We are now caring for 700 in the homes, including workers." Many in the audience responded generously to the financial needs of the homes.

He told the crowd, "The Jubilee Trio and I will be flying out of Corpus Christi tomorrow morning." The tour schedule would take them to Kansas City on Tuesday, the second of November, and end in Atlanta on Sunday, the ninth of November.

A winter Texan said, "Those groups sounded just like angels as they sang." Brother Roloff had often remarked, "They were far from angels when they came to the homes."

The crowd applauded Brother Roloff for his stand against state encroachment on the church and church ministries.

He reminded everyone of the importance of the governor's race and of voting the next day. He said he would vote the next morning before they took off on the tour. Everyone seemed to know that he preferred Governor Bill Clements over challenger Mark White.

When he arrived back in Corpus Christi that night, Brother Roloff recorded two broadcasts for later release on the Family Altar Program. He laid his financial burden before the radio audience. He said he had not personally accumulated one thing. "Yesterday we cleared out our personal bank account of fourteen hundred dollars and borrowed sixteen hundred dollars more. We gave it to the ministry to help somebody."

He played a recording of a song which he and Miss Frances had made years before entitled, "He Bore the Cross for Me." He gave tribute to Mrs. Frances Price (Miss

Frances) for her talent and many years of service. They sang, "I've heard His call, I owe my all. . . ."

In one of the messages recorded that night, he said, "This is a special day — this is a special broadcast." And, "If I had a thousand lives, I'd want them all to count in this kind of ministry." He said, "We're going on a long journey."

The Jubilee Trio sang "My God and I" which says in part, "My God and I walk through the fields together."

Cheryl Palmer was a member of the trio and a daughter of Raymond and Kaye Palmer who surrendered their lives to work with children. They later became the superintendents of the Rebekah Home for Girls. Cheryl gave her testimony. "I was saved when I was six years old and called to be a missionary when I was only nine. I got into sin that caused serious depression. It got worse until I didn't want to live anymore; then I overdosed. My parents came to my apartment and took me to the Jubilee Home. I was twenty-one years old. God gave me a second chance. He straightened out my life and let me work the last three months with the Apache Indians at the Regeneration Reservation in Arizona." She announced, "I'm on my way to a mansion in the sky," which was the cue for the trio to sing, "I'm on my way to a mansion in the sky. Well, I'm on my way to an everlasting bye and bye . . . ."

Enola Slade, from Durango, Colorado, a young lady in the trio, gave her testimony. "I got into trouble and started smoking dope and taking pills. . . ." She quoted Joshua 1:9 which says in part, ". . . be not afraid, neither be thou dismayed: for the Lord thy God is with thee whithersoever thou goest." "I am so thankful for the homes and for salvation. Please pray with me for my family that they, too, will come to know the Lord."

Sue Smith, from Omaha, Nebraska, another young lady in the trio, gave her testimony. "I was defeated and had gone through a series of twenty-three shock treatments. The Lord saved me and cured me when I came to the homes." Then she announced the next song, "As the Father hath sent me, so send I you."

The trio and Brother Roloff sang songs with the following messages: "Oh, joy, Oh, delight, should He come without dying." "Though the cost be great, I'll work for Thee." "Oh, Lord Jesus, how long, how long, ere we shout the glad song . . . Hallelujah, Hallelujah, Amen."

Brother Roloff reminded the girls again, "We're leaving on a long tour." And later when he said, "Girls, we've got a long journey ahead."

Brother Roloff's assistant, Brother Wiley Cameron, commented, "One of the last things he said just before leaving Corpus Christi was, 'This is going to be the greatest day of my life.'"

At about 9 A.M. Brother Roloff and the Jubilee Trio, along with Elaine Wingert, a supervisor from the homes, took off from Cuddihy Field, an old reclaimed military airstrip near the People's Baptist Church. His flight plan would take him over the Dawson, Texas, area — near the old farm place. He probably would have pointed down to show the young ladies in the plane just where he was born and raised. (There were thunderstorms in the area.)

He was being tracked on radar and radio from Houston Air Traffic Control Center. Brother Roloff contacted Houston with a request to go to fifteen thousand feet. Permission was granted.

A little later, Brother Roloff contacted Houston with a request to go higher to seventeen thousand feet. Permission was again given by Houston Air Traffic Control Center. He reported flying just above the clouds to which Houston replied, "Roger, that's O.K." Brother Roloff then said, "Thank you now." After a barometric pressure resetting on the altimeter Brother Roloff said, "Good day."

Houston reported that they lost contact with the Cessna 210 Roloff was flying at 10:18 A.M. The above radio transmissions are from an official copy of the transcriptions from the U.S. Department of Transportation, Federal Aviation Administration.

R.L. Lamb, a 79-year-old farmer, was picking beans in his garden. In a telephone interview, he said he heard a loud explosion he thought was either a gunshot or a plane breaking the sound barrier. A *Corpus Christi Caller Times* article read:

> "It was about three hours later that Lamb and his 71-year-old wife, Oma Dean, received a call from a reporter who said a plane had crashed near their home. They drove down the road to where they could see the wreckage of a plane lying in the middle of an open pasture owned by Eugene Pollard. The plane had gone down about three-quarters of a mile from Lamb's home."

Brother Roloff and the four precious young ladies died in the crash.

The location of the crash was three miles north of Normangee, Texas, near the Madison-Leon county line and about 110 miles north of Houston.

The last request recorded by Brother Roloff was to "go higher." His last recorded words were, "Thank you now," and "Good day."

54

National Reaction

As the news spread, Mrs. Roloff, the Roloff Evangelistic Enterprises' office, the church, and the Roloff Homes started receiving calls voicing disbelief. They came from everywhere. Brother Cameron, Alfred Edge, Miss Ida Cavitt, and the other directors of the ministry were in a state of shocked disbelief. Even those who were only friends of the ministry received calls from all over the nation, asking if they had heard the news and if it were true?

Many friends went to their spouses immediately because they did not want them to hear the news without some support.

"Heaven is a richer place for (Lester) Roloff's death, but we're certainly poorer here on earth," said Dr. Bob Jones III when he heard the news.

Dr. Jerry Falwell said, "I'm shocked; I considered Lester Roloff one of the great giants of this generation."

Texas Governor Clements called Roloff "a great Texan doing God's work."

Plans for the funeral to be held at the church were soon changed because of the response from across the nation. A larger facility was needed. Arrangements were made to use the Corpus Christi Memorial Coliseum.

The funeral service was conducted on the fifth of November. *The Corpus Christi Caller Times* reported:

The crowd of thousands at the funeral on Corpus Christi's bayfront couldn't have differed more widely. Its members were black, white, brown, old, young, and very young. Three-piece-suited men sat next to men wearing boots and faded shirts. . . .

The service began on a victorious note as Bill Harvey lead the entire congregation in singing "Living By Faith."

Curtis Hudson led in prayer. He said, "If measured by the people he reached, Brother Lester Roloff was one of the greatest giants of this and every generation."

Brother Cameron said, "Brother Roloff was a great soldier of the cross, and it is only fitting that two great servicemen will present the colors." Clebe McClary and Tim Lee — marines who were terribly injured in battle — presented the colors. Tim Lee lost both legs in battle, and Clebe McClary lost one arm, one eye, and partial use of his remaining arm and legs. Both men are very active in serving the Lord. They presented a flag saved from a battlefield in Vietnam. It was shattered by bullet holes, but it never went down. The flag was draped over the casket. Brother Cameron placed Brother Roloff's Bible on the flag. Next to the casket (on an easel) was a framed color picture of Brother Roloff. Below, flowers lined the stage front.

During his message, Dr. Bob Jones, Jr., said:

Our lives are immortal until our work is done. The Lord's timing is always perfect, and I cannot find myself weeping when God's man enters the gates of glory. That's not an occasion for sorrow; that's an occasion for rejoicing.

He (Lester Roloff) bore the brunt of the battle. He stood in the gap. He never retreated. He knew what it was to be lied about, slandered, and opposed by the wrong kind of preachers and the wrong kind of public officials.

He was a man who — what he began he finished —

and his motivation was always love. It is strange today that a man who has conviction and stands by the truth and will not back down for the defense of the Word of God is somehow an unloving person. But, my friend, a man who stands by the Word of God today is motivated by the Word of God. He will not surrender because the truth is too important to lay on the altar of sacrifice. And those who love Christ cannot do other than press the battle. He was motivated by love for young people, for young men and young women. How many thousands his life has touched.

When I think of Lester, I think of his uniqueness. You know it's awfully interesting to watch a young preacher try to imitate some older preacher whom he admires. He seeks out all of his eccentricities and things that are spots upon his ministry and imitates them because they are obvious. But, the things that make a man's ministry great are things that are not on the surface and not so easily seen. You must look at the many hours he spends on his knees in prayer, the time he spends in preparation, the moments he gives in counseling those whom he loves and those who look to him for care and for protection. It is not the style of his preaching that makes him great, it's the burden of his heart. And I hope that as we look toward the future, if God tarries, that those who follow after Brother Roloff will not try to be like him; that is impossible. No man can imitate greatness successfully because greatness is something that comes out of the nature of the man himself. I hope they will instead ask for the double portion and for his mantle to fall upon them — his love for the Lord, his love for young people, his faithfulness in service, and his sweet and joyful spirit in the midst of persecution.

We've lost a great man. And as they said over the

281

grave of Caesar, "We shall not see his life again, but we shall see him again" — one day in the presence of the Lord.

Down here he was *in* Christ; now he is *with* Christ. And someday all the saints of God together with him shall be *like* Christ; for we shall see Him as He is, and that is the only thing that is going to bring perfect satisfaction to all of us.

We used to sing a song we don't hear so much anymore. *Be like Jesus this my song, in the home and in the throng; be like Jesus all day long.* . . . Every child of God who is surrendered likes to pray that prayer in his heart; but as long as we are in the flesh, we can never be completely like Him. But someday when He shall appear, we can say with the psalmist, "I shall be satisfied, when I awake, with Thy likeness." There is nothing beyond that, nothing greater, nothing more joyful, nothing to crown the soul with delight as to look on Jesus and know finally by divine grace, we've become like Him. Down here we see Him by faith — over there, face-to-face. Down here we labor in the bonds of the flesh and the limitations of our humanity. But over there we shall run and not be weary, we shall walk and not faint. And we shall serve Him in the fullness of wisdom and of strength, breathing the air of Heaven and inspired by the music of the redeemed — and that is always a song of glory to the Lamb, the One who washed us from our sins in His own blood. He has made us to be kings and priests unto God. To Him be glory.

Finally, I was thinking as I flew down here today, I wonder what judgment waits upon Texas. God sometimes takes His man out of the way so that the judgment of God can begin to move. And there are those who shall feel, in this place, the judgment of God for their opposition — not just to God's man, but to the Lord Jesus Christ and His Word that were upheld and exalted by a man who loved the Lord with all his heart and who would not bow the knee.

Thank God he went to jail; but, like Paul, he came out of jail with greater power and greater strength. And I believe that God has removed this man now, that some elected officials in this state who have tried to hinder the Word of God shall know the lashings of God's judgment. And I go away praying for God's mercy upon this state and upon its public officials.

You have recently elected some masterpieces of depravity. Some good men, but some men who stand with apparently no fear of God or God's judgment, desiring to hinder the work of God and exalt in its place those things that will take away God's blessings and bring God's judgment upon them and upon the people.

So my heart is very heavy today as I think of this great state and what may lie ahead for you. I wonder if Brother Roloff hasn't been removed, this one who by his prayer held back God's judgment, that God may move in the power of His wrath and make bare His mighty arm.

Thank God for this man; thank God for all he stood for. And thank God for the assurance that God, who raised him up, shall raise up someone else, not like him — for though the warrior falls, the battle goes on; though the soldier lies in rest, the conflict must be pressed. The days are evil, the time is short before the Lord comes. May we gird up our loins and draw forth the sword of the Spirit and go out and do exploits for God remembering this man and God's blessing upon him. May we give all honor and glory to the Lord Jesus, Whom he loved and Whom he served.

Brother Cameron asked everyone who was presently at the homes to stand. Hundreds of people stood and were applauded.

The Rebekah Choir sang "That's Just What Heaven Means to Me."

The Lighthouse Ensemble sang "God of Our Fathers."

All the preachers, missionaries, and evangelists were asked to stand. Several hundred stood to a rousing applause.

Dr. Harold Clayton then spoke with a voice that was nearly overwhelmed with emotion:

Here is one Texan who was Brother Roloff's friend. My wife and I went to Waco years ago to an old-fashioned Premillennial Bible Conference. We met Brother Roloff for the first time. He preached a sermon entitled "And the Mule Walked On." He yanked his coat off every time he preached. For about five years after that I yanked my coat off every time I preached. I know Dr. Jones said we are not supposed to imitate him, but I couldn't help it.

When our church burned in 1975, the phone rang and someone began singing, "In shady green pastures so rich and so sweet, God leads His dear children along. . . ."

"Is . . . that . . . you . . . Brother Roloff?" I asked through my tears. He encouraged me a few minutes and prayed for me.

He was a friend of young people. He was a friend of *down-and-outers*. He was a friend of God.

The Anchor Home boys sang "That I May Be Like Jesus" and "Oh, to Be Like Thee."

Brother Cameron held up a letter Brother Roloff had dictated just before takeoff which he called a "Letter to Preachers." He read the letter in which Brother Roloff reminded the preachers there were 700 people on the 500-acre campus. He told them he had just borrowed $200,000. He said he would rather die for the "Least, Last, and the Lost" than to retreat. He said he had been given trouble by the DHR but that he was looking to the DDR (Department of Divine Resources). He told of a girl who recently had committed suicide after they had to turn her away.

He said, "I'm tired and more weary than I've been in all of my 68 years." He told the preachers they would have to help him if he was to reach the "Pitiful, Passing Parade of the Perishing."

Brother Bill Reese said that the preacher had told him once, "If you ever hear that I've gone down, that I'm dead; don't you believe it." He said Brother Lester had confided in him, "I'm so tired, I'm so weary, the burden is so great, so heavy — I've done all I know to do — but God is great." Brother Reese said, "Now the battle is over, and Lester Roloff is wearing a crown."

Dr. Bob Gray's Associate Pastor, Brother Lenny Willinger, said that Dr. Gray was not present because he had a previous engagement. He said Dr. Gray had wrestled with the decision, but that Brother Roloff helped him make the decision. He said Lester was preaching in his church when he received a message that his mother was dying, and if he wanted to see her alive, he must come at once. He stayed and preached. He said that is what his mother would want him to do. His mother died the following day. Dr. Gray said that helped him make his decision. He knew Brother Roloff would want him to honor his present commitment which was raising funds for an orphanage. He said, "Brother Roloff has spoken in our Annual Bible Conference for 24 straight years." He expressed his grief in the loss of his dear friend.

Brother Cameron asked the Jubilee Ensemble to sing. He

first paid tribute to Miss Elaine Wingert, Miss Cheryl Palmer, Miss Susan Smith, and Miss Enola Slade, who lost their lives in the plane crash. Three of them were part of the Jubilee Home's young ladies. The ensemble sang with great emotion: "If We Could See Beyond Today."

The City of Refuge men sang "In the House of the Lord."

The crowd was reminded by Brother Cameron that Brother Roloff had said when the first City of Refuge began in Lee county, Texas, "If God will save one old drunk, it will be worth it."

Dr. Lee Roberson's son, John Roberson, represented him. John said it was not possible for his father to be there. He brought out three impressions from the book of James that depicted Brother Roloff. He said there was nothing fancy about him; there was nothing fake about him; and he kept himself unspotted from the world.

He read a telegram from his father, Dr. Lee Roberson, which said:

Allow me to pay my respects to the man with less fear and more faith than any man in this twentieth century. That man was Lester Roloff. He feared neither man nor machine. He feared neither poverty nor plenty. His faith in God made him courageous, loyal, and daring. His compassion was boundless.

"And this is the victory that overcometh the world, even our faith."

The Highland Park Baptist Church and the Tennessee Temple University join together in sending our sympathy to Mrs. Roloff, daughters, and hundreds in the Roloff Homes. Sincerely, Lee Roberson.

Three members of the Honey Bee Quartet were present. They sang "I Want to Stroll over Heaven with You."

The Men's Trio sang one of their newer songs that Brother Roloff liked, "I'll Be Home before Dark."

Dr. Hyles gave a talk based on Hebrews 11:40: "God having provided some better thing for us, that they without us should not be made perfect." He compared the Christian experience to a relay race where one runner takes the baton from the previous runner. But, he said, the race is not won until the last runner runs. The previous runners are at the finish line cheering the others on. "Brother Lester is there on the finish line, and there is a heap of cheering going on."

Dozens of young men came during the invitation to surrender their lives to full-time service for the Lord. These were encouraged to take the mantle of this great leader and do even greater things for God. The young men were told, "Take the baton from him and run your best — no one ever ran a faster lap than Brother Roloff."

Christians were encouraged to rededicate their lives to Christ as the thing that Brother Roloff would most want.

It seemed to be a consensus among the speakers that one reason God took Brother Roloff was that He did not want him to face the disappointment of seeing his friend and supporter, Governor Bill Clements, defeated. His challenger was the Attorney General who always seemed available to enforce bureaucratic rules against the homes and ministry. Governor Clements was defeated on the same day of Brother Roloff's death.

People came from many parts of the nation to the funeral. Many wept during the service. The funeral service ended quietly with hundreds kneeling before the stage. Brother Roloff's widow, Marie, and their grown daughters, Elizabeth Ann and Pamela, were escorted to a waiting limousine for the drive to the cemetery, west of the city.

A request was made by the Corpus Christi Police Department during the funeral services for people not to go to the cemetery due to the many vehicles that would jam some main streets of the city. However, thousands did join the procession. Men were enlisted from the Roloff Homes, located directly across the highway from the cemetery, to help control the traffic and the crowd. The *Caller Times* reported:

Roloff's entourage arrived shortly before 5 P.M. led by five black limousines and a black hearse. Also, in the procession were 10 buses bearing students from five of the pastor's homes for children. The pallbearers carried the modest-colored bronze casket from the hearse to the gravesite, followed by the evangelist's immediate survivors. When the family assembled under the green canopy, the throng surrounded the plot to join the mourning ritual. The minister's words were drowned in the monotone drones of two circling helicopters.

The service lasted 10 minutes, ending with a prayer for members of Roloff's family, who were ushered from the site, leaving the crowd staring at the casket adorned with a blue ribbon that threaded through a bouquet of red and white carnations.

The autumn sun was setting with an orange hue in the South Texas sky. The sun was also setting in the hearts of those who lingered in that lonely cemetery. A champion had fallen, a defender of the faith who would never be replaced. Possibly some brave, dedicated leader would emerge, but there would never be another Lester Roloff. He, no doubt, was cut from the cloth of God's noblemen. This man was the hero of those for whom he gave his life. Some were saying and many more were thinking: *Where would I be today if it had not been for this man? Who else would have stopped to dress my wounds? Who would have taken me to the inn? Who would have paid for everything I needed physically, while, under the preaching of His Word, God was restoring my soul? Others had said they loved me, but this is the only man who proved it. When no one else would even come close to me or touch me, he put his arms around me, lifted me out of sin's gutter, and led me to the very Source of that love. Thank You, Jesus, for living in Lester Roloff and reproducing Your life in me.*

The void remained for many as they drove slowly past Memory Gardens solemnly looking toward Roloff's grave. Many seemed to be thinking as dusk was falling, *So long for now, my dear brother, we'll see you in the morning.*

On the flight to Corpus Christi for the funeral, Brother Bill Harvey composed the following poem:

BROTHER LESTER'S LAST FLIGHT?

He took his last flight?
Oh, not at all.
He preached the rapture,
As I recall,
And he'll be true to what
He preached,
And soon be raised with
Those he reached.

He filed his flight plan
Years ago
His time-tanks were full,
He was ready to go
His route is direct
To Heaven above
No side trips for funds
To prove people's love.

His last flight, you say?
No, he'll fly again
Without a prop or motor then,
And there'll be a cloud,
But he won't mind;
His Lord will be in it,
His pilot so kind.

Following are selected verses from a song which was one of Brother Roloff's favorites:

THE LITTLE HOUSE ON HALLELUJAH STREET

There's a house in Grumbler's Alley where I lived some years ago,
And the walls were swiftly falling to decay.
And the yard was full of thistles, and the roof was rotted so,
That the storms beat in upon me night and day.

Then the Spirit came and told me of a wonderful abode
Where from wind and storm I'd find a safe retreat,
So the Saviour sent His moving van and He took me up the road,
To the little house on Hallelujah Street.

Now this house is nice and cozy, and its walls so warm and tight,
And the Landlord doesn't charge me any rent.
There's a garden in connection, filled with flowers gay and bright,
Where so many golden hours I have spent.

Here the landscape is so lovely, and the songbirds sing with glee,
And I'm never hungry for good things to eat.
And I'm never never lonely, for the Saviour dines with me,
At the little house on Hallelujah Street.

I shall ne'er forget the day that I moved from sin away,
And secured a change of address so complete.
Since that moment, without fail, I've been getting all my mail
At the little house on Hallelujah Street.

55

Lost His Case?

In retrospect God probably did not want Lester Roloff to suffer another crushing blow to the ministry as happened on October 7, 1985, some three years after his death. The Supreme Court refused to hear the church's appeal, saying that no pertinent facts had changed in the case that would make it of national significance. The State of Texas had successfully commandeered the authority of a church in its ministry of helping young people into which God calls all churches. The Supreme Court decided that was not a violation of the Constitution.

The Pilgrims and the writers of the Constitution and its By-Laws would surely have caused a national commotion if they had been here and heard the supreme overlords of justice flaunt their agenda of constitutional circumvention. They allowed a state seizure of authority over a church ministry without so much as a hearing. The state took another giant step forward in its quest for power.

There is in the making a grisly, rear-end collision. The news media furnished the bureaucrats with propaganda channels as they seized control over a church's child-care ministry. Surely they knew that bureaucrats have an insatiable love for power. The freedom of the press is no more protected than freedom of religion. Although the news media are naively comfortable now as liberal bedfellows with the bureaucrats, they need to check their rear-view mirror to see who that is coming up behind them so fast. Concerning *public opinion* about the freedom of the press, the public is being conditioned daily to say, "It couldn't happen to a nicer bunch."

Some will probably say, "The Roloff case was a matter of reasonable concern for the care of children." Let the courts themselves respond to this. The Associated Press dateline from Corpus Christi, Texas, on Oct. 8, 1985, read: "The issue is not whether People's Baptist Church is performing a service that is beneath (below) licensing standards. The three homes have a good record of high quality service." This is a quote from the Texas Supreme Court ruling. The case was clearly a bureaucratic grab for power.

Sour grapes? Hardly. The Beatitudes instruct Christians to expect these things. They are to fight a good fight, and though misunderstood and persecuted, they are not to lose their joy — they can still be happy. Christ said, "Rejoice and be exceeding glad: for great is your reward in heaven: for so persecuted they the prophets which were before you" (Matthew 5:12). "Blessed are ye, when men shall revile you, and persecute you, and shall say all manner of evil against you falsely, for My sake" (Matthew 5:11). Brother Roloff said, "If Christians really knew how all of this is going to turn out for them, they would throw their hats over the windmill and shout Hallelujah!"

This has been one of the most blatant cases in American history of persecution against a man who practiced righteousness in every area of his life. He was hated by the evildoers and the do-gooders who believed good could not be accomplished without Caesar's approval. "I am on the winning side," Brother Roloff often said. What did he mean by that? Another Beatitude says, "Blessed are they which are persecuted for righteousness' sake, for theirs is the Kingdom of Heaven" (Matthew 5:10).

While this "loser" is enjoying the Kingdom of Heaven for eternity, what does the Bible say about those who had a hand in closing the homes? The Rebekah and Anchor Homes' only purpose was to lead children to Christ and rescue them from drugs, alcohol, and other habits of self-destruction. The Bible's most serious warnings are addressed to those who offend these believers: "But whoso shall offend one of these little ones which believe in Me, it were better for him that a millstone were hanged about his neck, and that he were drowned in the depth of the sea" (Matthew 18:6).

Does the Bible address those who viciously attacked Brother Roloff personally? "Woe unto the world because of offenses! For it must needs be that offenses come; but woe to that man by whom the offense cometh" (Matthew 18:7).

Never be guilty of thinking Lester Roloff ultimately lost his case. Do not waste your time feeling sorry for him. His is the Kingdom of Heaven. He would be the first to say, concerning the Constitution bashing by the Supreme Court, the Bible bashing by the State of Texas, and the Roloff bashing by the news media, "Father, forgive them for they know not what they do." Every Christian who has seen the injustices that drove this man to his death should be quick to pray that the offenders will have their eyes opened and will find Christ as Savior.

Brother Roloff finally confessed that he was guilty beyond question. He was guilty of *love in the first degree.*

Mama and Papa Roloff would be pleased to know that in living for Christ, he played for keeps. He "played for keeps" with his soul. He "played for keeps" with the souls of tens of thousands of defeated men, women, boys, and girls. He "played for keeps" with millions of listeners to the Family Altar Program. One of his favorite songs was "He's the Keeper of My Soul." When Jesus Christ saves someone, it is for keeps.

Brother Roloff is not dead. He lives in the lives of all

293

those who found new life in Christ through his ministries. He did not live in vain; new life is still being found by many because Brother Roloff was obedient to his heavenly calling. The Roloff Homes in Corpus Christi continue to win many men and women to Christ. They continue to work with children. However, one or both of the child's parents must remain at the homes with the child. Child-care homes were spun off from the Roloff ministries to other states as workers resigned and left Texas for friendlier environments. The Regeneration Reservation in Arizona is a particularly strong example of the continuing voice of Brother Roloff as it expands regularly with excellent facilities for reaching more North American Indians. All of these works came about by one man's faith and dedication to his God-given vision.

Lester Roloff's voice continues literally today as he preaches on the Family Altar Program. The program takes the gospel via radio waves across America and around the world. He lives through all the gospel preachers and missionaries who continue to preach today because they were called by God while under his ministry.

56

What Caused The Crash?

Much speculation has surfaced since that fateful Tuesday, November 2, 1982, as to the cause of the fatal crash. It is almost certain that weather was not the primary cause of the crash. Several of that vintage aircraft had previously crashed due to structural failure. Design problems were proven in enough cases just like this one, where the tail section came off, that Cessna paid the Roloff Evangelistic Enterprises, Inc., for the aircraft. Undisclosed amounts were also given to the families of those who lost their lives in the crash. Most of the amounts given by Cessna were unselfishly assigned by the affected families to the Roloff Evangelistic Enterprises as a memorial to their dear loved ones, to carry on the work for which the four young ladies and Brother Roloff died.

Epilogue

Many sincere Christians have not understood why Brother Roloff refused to apply for a state license for the youth homes. Some Christians even joined the state in its fight against the Roloff Homes. They said their facility had a license and they were never bothered by the state in their day-to-day operations. Others with state licenses reported having many problems. Several turned their licenses back to the state during the attack on the Roloff Homes.

You will be interested to know what happened at a proposed Boy's Ranch planned by Lester Roloff. A down payment for a ranch was given by a lady who was a Family Altar Program listener. The lady lived in the Rio Grande Valley, not far from the 327 acre ranch.

A Board of Directors was formed specifically for that work. The reason for a separate Board was that Brother Roloff wanted that work to be a trial run with the state to see if there was any possibility of running a licensed home according to his Bible convictions.

Brother Roloff, this writer, and four others were on that Board. They chose me to approach the Welfare Department Child-Care Division and apply for a license.

An appointment was made with the appropriate representative in Corpus Christi, Texas, where license applications for child-care facilities were handled.

At the appointed time I was ushered into the man's office where I was welcomed and seated across the desk from him.

"What can I do for you?" he asked.

I informed him that I was there to apply for a license for

a child-care facility which would be located north of Edinburg, Texas.

"O.K., we will need to get some information about your organization," he said. "What is the name of the proposed owner?"

"The facility will be owned and operated by the Roloff Evangelistic Enterprises, Inc.," I replied.

The man pushed his writing pad back and leaned back in his chair. "You are wasting your time," he announced curtly.

"What do you mean?" I asked in wonder.

"I mean, you are wasting your time because you will never get a license," he said.

"Surely, you have an explanation for that kind of response."

"Yes, I do," he said coldly. "You see, we already know about this Roloff organization, and we know they use the Bible in their program. We do not believe the Bible, and we will not allow it to be used in any program for a child-care facility."

"That's it?" I asked.

He said, "That's it."

Standing to my feet, I said, "I can't say you have been helpful, but you have certainly been candid with me. All I can do is report to Brother Roloff what you have said."

"That is fine. If Mr. Roloff has any questions, have him call me."

I did not know what to expect when I reported to Brother Roloff. His response was a calm, matter-of-fact reply: "If that is their rule and that is their attitude, then there will be no licenses, but we will continue with our plan to start a boy's ranch on that property."

Some cattle were donated and placed on the ranch. A young couple moved into a mobile home on the property in

1961. Plans were begun for building facilities and enlisting workers.

A few months later, the lady who had furnished the down payment for the property called me while I was in the office where I worked near Mission, Texas. She said, "Bobby, I'm sick."

Thinking it might be some physical problem because of her advanced age, I became concerned and asked, "What is the matter? What can I do to help you?"

She said, "There is nothing you can do. There is nothing anyone can do. I just found out that Brother Roloff is a crook and I have lost my money. And the title to the ranch is in the Roloff Enterprises' name."

"Who told you he is a crook?" I asked.

"There is a group of men who visited me and told me all about him," she said.

"Will you give me the names of the men?"

"No!" she said. "They don't want their names mentioned."

"Will you ask them to meet with me, or better, ask them to meet with Brother Roloff and make their accusations directly to him as the Bible instructs?"

"Oh, they wouldn't do that," she said. "They don't want this to become a public scandal."

"They will not handle this the way the Bible instructs Christians, and yet you believe them?" I asked.

"Yes, I believe them," she said.

"Why are you calling me instead of Brother Roloff?"

"Well, I want you to try to get my money back — or the property. I don't want to talk with him because I don't want him talking me out of this. I have my mind made up."

"What do you plan to do with the property if you get it back?" I asked.

"I plan to give it to another group that promises to get

something started on it right away," she said. "You see, I am getting to be an old lady, and I want to see something done for children on that property before I die."

"Is it the same group which is giving you this information about Brother Roloff?" I asked.

"Yes, it is."

"They don't want their names mentioned, and you are sure they would not meet with Brother Roloff. Is that right?"

"That's right, Bobby."

"I will talk with Brother Roloff, and either he or I will call you very soon."

"Tell him it will not do any good for him to call me. My mind is fixed on what I want to do," she said with determination.

"I will tell him today, and will let you know what he says."

I did call Brother Roloff that day. We talked for only a few minutes. Then he said, "She is on the Board of the Boy's Ranch there. If she believes what she has been told, I would never be able to work with her. Tell her I will talk to the attorney today, and the property will be signed over to her tomorrow."

When I called her about an hour after she had first called me, she was elated and could hardly believe what she was hearing. I told her, "I have known Brother Roloff for fifteen years, and he is the most honest man I have ever known. Remember this; you have been misled — but not by Brother Roloff."

There is no Christian work on that property at the time of this writing — thirty-two years later.

When the ranch was transferred back to the lady, I believe Brother Roloff was thinking what I was: *This is the Lord's way of letting him know that he was out of God's will when he sought permission from the state or anyone else before rescuing criminal youth, dope addicts, and alcoholics as God led him to do. Time had been wasted. Souls slipped away that could have been rescued.*

I often wondered why he never used that experience as one of his reasons for refusing to seek a license on the other homes. I never heard him mention it publicly. We later discussed it privately because the lady demanded rent for the pasture while it was in Brother Roloff's control. True to form, he paid dearly.

Now, after watching the stand he took for an exception to state licensing for his ministry, I believe he was convicted and looked at it as if he had betrayed God by compromising his conscience. Remember, his homes were unique. They dealt with kids on drugs and those who were in trouble with the law. He believed in his heart those kids could not be dealt with using the same methods as noncriminal youth.

It is mentioned here to show the readers there were valid reasons, other than the Constitution, why he knew he could not be unequally yoked with unbelieving overseers in an intensive care type facility for hardened youth.

There are some licensed child-care facilities in Texas that use the Bible in their programs. I have only reported what the official said to me when I attempted to apply for a license. They do not differentiate between homes that deal with criminal youth and those that do not. We are thankful the Welfare Department was apparently thwarted in their plan to totally outlaw the Bible in child-care facilities.

The DHR has had input from an organization of licensed child-care facilities. We are thankful for the success of that organization and for any homes that continue to use the Bible in their programs. We are sincerely thankful for those who are being led to the Lord through these homes.

District Judge Joe B. Evans of Edinburg, Texas, said an

exception should be made to the license requirement for the Roloff Homes due to the type of children with whom they worked. He had sent several to the homes and was impressed with the results.

Even after the Supreme Court case was lost, judges continued to send children to the homes. They said they were allowed to do that on a conservator arrangement. This, too, was eventually blocked through the insistence of the heartless bureaucrats and their tax-paid lawyers. Their power meant more to them than providing criminal youths one last chance.

Can anyone in clear conscience say Lester Roloff was wrong? There were tens of thousands of rebellious children and young people won to the Lord. Most had no other choice but to go to the Roloff Homes or to prison. The ultimate question is "Did God honor his faith?"

Thousands of parents will attest to the fact that their children were rescued because of this man's obedience to God. Black crepe has been hung on Heaven's gates as he predicted would happen if the homes were closed by the Supreme Court. Thousands of youths are now going to prison who would have been sent to the homes. Most of them will never enter Heaven's gates. We should pray for those who are responsible for the black crepe because as Brother Roloff said, "There will be a judgment."

After having known Lester Roloff for more than 47 years, I am convinced he was a man whose faith was in God alone. By faith he spent his endless energy and gave his vibrant life doing God's bidding.

No other man in our times has come close to him in proving what can be wrought through faith alone. Even so, he prayed continually that God would increase his faith. He was a faithful representative of Christ. His methods of ministering were learned from God's Word. He trusted God

301

to bless the ministry. Multitudes can attest to the fact that God was faithful to His believing servant, Lester Roloff.